Sermons For Advent/Christmas/Epiphany Based On Gospel Texts For Cycle C

*Deep Joy For
A Shallow World*

Richard A. Wing

CSS Publishing Company, Inc., Lima, Ohio

SERMONS FOR ADVENT/CHRISTMAS/EPIPHANY BASED ON GOSPEL TEXTS
FOR CYCLE C: DEEP JOY FOR A SHALLOW WORLD

Copyright © 1997 by
CSS Publishing Company, Inc.
Lima, Ohio

All rights reserved. No part of this publication may be reproduced in any manner whatsoever without the prior permission of the publisher, except in the case of brief quotations embodied in critical articles and reviews. Inquiries should be addressed to: Permissions, CSS Publishing Company, Inc., P.O. Box 4503, Lima, Ohio 45802-4503.

Scripture quotations are from the *New Revised Standard Version of the Bible*, copyright 1989 by the Division of Christian Education of the National Council of the Churches of Christ in the USA. Used by permission.

Library of Congress Cataloging-in-Publication Data

Wing, Richard A.
   Sermons for Advent/Christmas/Epiphany based on Gospel texts for Cycle C : deep joy for a shallow world / Richard A. Wing.
     p.   cm.
   ISBN 0-7880-1033-6
   1. Advent sermons. 2. Christmas sermons. 3. Epiphany season — Sermons. 4. Sermons, American. 5. Bible. N.T. Gospels—Sermons. I. Title.
BV40.W54   1997
252'.61—dc21
                                                           97-9973
                                                                CIP

This book is available in the following formats, listed by ISBN:
   0-7880-1033-6   Book
   0-7880-1090-5   Mac
   0-7880-1091-3   IBM 3 1/2
   0-7880-1092-1   Sermon Prep

PRINTED IN U.S.A.

*For my Mother
Lois Wing
with the deepest
gratitude
for her deep faith*

Editor's Note Regarding The Lectionary

During the past two decades there has been an attempt to move in the direction of a uniform lectionary among various Protestant denominations.

Preaching on the same scripture lessons every Sunday is a step in the right direction of uniting Christians of many faiths. If we are reading the same scriptures together, we may also begin to accomplish other achievements. Our efforts will be strengthened through our unity.

Beginning with Advent 1995 The Evangelical Lutheran Church in America dropped its own lectionary schedule and adopted the Revised Common Lectionary.

Reflecting this change, resources published by CSS Publishing Company put their major emphasis on the Revised Common Lectionary texts for the church year.

Table Of Contents

Preface   7

Introduction   9

Advent 1   11
   Made New By Interior Design
   Luke 21:25-36

Advent 2   17
   Made New By Getting Lost
   Luke 3:1-6

Advent 3   23
   Made New By 180 Degrees
   Luke 3:7-18

Advent 4   33
   Made New By Taking A Different Road Home
   Luke 1:39-45

Christmas Eve/Day   39
   Yours For The Asking
   Luke 2:1-20

Christmas 1   43
   Living By The Calendar Instead Of The Clock
   Luke 2:41-52

Epiphany   53
   Kneeling And Redirection
   Matthew 2:1-12

Baptism Of The Lord   59
   Echoes
   Luke 3:15-17, 21-22

Epiphany 2   63
   The Best For Last
   John 2:1-11

Epiphany 3   69
   Deep Joy For A Shallow World
   Luke 4:14-21

Epiphany 4   75
   Edges
   Luke 4:21-30

Epiphany 5   79
   Is It Better To Catch Or Be Caught?
   Luke 5:1-11

Epiphany 6   83
   Flatliners
   Luke 6:17-26

Epiphany 7   91
   Love Your Enemies — It Will Drive Them Crazy
   Luke 6:27-38

The Transfiguration Of The Lord   101
   Getting The Face We Deserve
   Luke 9:28-36 (37-43, 51)

Preface

Anyone who knows book writing knows that such a project is not a solo performance, but a group project.

The group that has been midwife to the compilation of these sermons is, first of all, the marvelous congregation of First Community Church, whose faithful listening and kind critiques have been indispensable in the making of this book. Secondly, it includes the faithful editing by Mary Jane Carroll, Nancy Baker, Mary Sims, and Colleen Knapp, along with the wonderful work of my administrative assistant, Jeanne Blair. They are word crafters extraordinaire!

Finally, I thank my wife Shirley Evans Wing, whose consistent encouragement and measurement of my work is my single greatest inspiration.

Introduction

How is it possible for us to receive the first steps of the Good News of Jesus Christ as if for the first time? How can we hear the words, as Marcus Borg says, "Again for the first time"?

Familiarity breeds contempt and complacency. Familiarity with anyone or anything, including scripture, breeds a false sense of ownership which dulls the power that was intended when the word was given.

Peter made a great confession about Jesus being the Christ. Just after that confession, Jesus says that he will suffer and die at the hands of religious people. Peter takes Jesus aside and "rebukes him." Jesus in turn does the same to Peter and tells Peter that he has a problem. Jesus says, "You are thinking not as God thinks, but as human beings do" (Mark 8:33b).

As we begin the church year with Advent and move swiftly to the season of Epiphany, perhaps we can pause long enough and pray that we might receive these words (1) as if for the first time, and (2) as words from God, who thinks differently than humans.

May you be blessed on this journey where we discover that we are made new, not by ownership or our own efforts, but by interior design by the hand and grace of God.

Made New
By Interior Design

Advent 1   **Luke 21:25-36**

Exterior design is changing everywhere in this season of Advent. The exterior designs are nice, but they will do us no ultimate good because in the end it is interior design that counts. The new interior design will not be the result of something we do, but the result of something we allow to have happen to us.

I assure you of this: God desires to do something inside us. God desires for something in the interior of our lives to be made new in this season. And there is the possibility that we might miss that crossing point.

There is help from our text. In this text, Jesus, at the end of his ministry, gives us advice that we can apply to the moment we anticipate his birth. The words of Jesus, taken out of context, can help us in this Advent adventure. Jesus said, "Observe, watch, get ready." He said that we should guard our hearts against waste and worry. This is the soundest advice that we could get as we enter this season.

I saw a bumper sticker which read, "Happiness is an inside job." I'm here to tell you that Advent is, too. What happens on the exterior is cosmetic and delightful but has limitations. What happens on the interior will occur when we choose to allow God to do something within us. That something has eternal value.

There are many barriers to our being made new by interior design in this Advent season.

Tears can be a barrier to Advent. In this season there will be tears of joy and tears of pain. In many homes across America, there will be gatherings in which a grandfather will look around the room at his children and grandchildren. At 85 years of age, he is aware that life is precious and short. At his age, he will realize how lucky he is to see everyone seated around him in relative peace and harmony. And he will cry. Those tears will be of deep joy. The family will not violate the moment by asking him why he is crying. They will understand. There will be wonderful tears of joy in this season.

There will also be tears of pain. Please trust this: *whatever you are feeling as we come into this season, you will feel it more intensely.* People who are up are really up. People who are down really feel down. We feel more intensely whatever we bring to the season.

Those who are in pain will have a special task before them. They, like Jacob wrestling the angel, will need to hold their pain down to the ground until they are blessed, not by the pain, but through the pain. We will pray for the courage to wrestle our pain to the ground until we are blessed.

Scott Peck was seated with a group listening intently to a woman describe in terrible detail the pain in her life. After she was through, Dr. Peck said quietly, "I am crying with one eye." He went on to explain that one eye of his was crying for the obvious pain that she was going through. The other eye, he said, was dry and gladdened by the fact that she had the courage to wrestle that pain to the ground until she was made stronger by it, rather than defeated by it.

So, bring your tears to Advent. Bring to this place the things you have lost, the things you are sorry for and the things you have not forgiven in yourself even though God has long ago forgiven you. The promise of God is that your tears will be transformed to triumph if you come to this place and grieve your own way and refuse to allow yourself to be fixed by the advice of others. By our learning to sit closely to each other in silence, God does the healing that we need so desperately. Tears can be a barrier to Advent. God can make them a bridge.

Anxiety can be another barrier to Advent. In our text, Jesus speaks of the "distress of the nations" and "people fainting with fear and dread of what is coming on the world." Jesus describes an anxiety that comes upon us when the transience of the world overwhelms us. Jesus would say that our anxiety is a sign of our help drawing near. Jesus would want us to know that "our extremity is God's opportunity." You know that the Chinese symbols for "crisis" and "opportunity" are the same symbol. Jesus knew that same anxiety.

I like John Cooper, the Ohio State University football coach, for many reasons, but especially for this one. As he was being interviewed once about a player who was in trouble with the law, a reporter asked if Cooper was going to kick the player off the team. He said, "No, I am not going to kick him off, because if I kick him off I can't help him. We are in the business of helping young people grow up, and you can't do that by turning them away when they make a mistake."

That is good news for those growing up, and that attitude is especially good news at Advent. We know in our hearts that we are changed for the better, not by persons who dump us in the midst of our mistakes, but by the ones who stand by us in our stupidity until the light of new sanity dawns upon us. Those who do this in our lives are gifts from God. The love of God is the kind that cares for us just as we are and not as we ought to be. In time, we become the way we are treated, not the way we deserve to be treated. This is God's finest gift. So, "watch — for your anxiety is God's opportunity."

During the Civil War, Mary Chestnut wrote a diary. She wrote it with great anxiety. As she witnessed Sherman's march to the sea, she wrote of a "solid column leaving not so much as a blade of grass behind; a howling wilderness, land laid waste, dust and ashes." This was her anxiety. But she failed to write about others' opportunity. If she were to have told all, she would have included the fact that "the slaves were dancing in the streets." One person's anxiety can be another's answer to the deepest desire of the heart.

Depression can be another barrier to Advent. Without oversimplifying, it appears to me that there are basically two kinds of depression. The first is the very understandable kind. I talked with a woman recently who had been married for over fifty years. Her husband died. She went through a period of depression. This is not hard to understand. Her loss led her into a depression that she could not get around, but had to get through.

There is a second kind of depression that seems to be chemical in nature. Some people have an imbalance in their systems that makes them feel as if there is a great cloud over their heads even if they have everything and every cause to be happy. Because there is nothing apparent to be depressed about, a double bind occurs. The person has no reason to be depressed and has everything that should make one happy and is still depressed. Thank God we have lived long enough to know that something chemical is happening here which needs the good guidance of a competent psychiatrist who will both counsel and use medication as needed.

Dietrich Bonhoeffer experienced the kind of depression that we can understand. This Lutheran pastor, who opposed the Nazis, was finally captured and brought to a prison camp. His captors told him that he would be executed and, in fact, he was. As he waited with tranquillity at times and depression at other times, he wrote:

> *Depression is loyalty's hour — the hour when mother, lover, friend, brother, cover over calamity, till it is **transfigured by gentle cosmic light!***

That is our deepest desire whether we know it or not: that somewhere in this season we are blessed and bathed in "gentle cosmic light" that shows the way through the inevitable darkness that comes with living on this earth.

I have read about a depressed songwriter who battled the successes of the past and a fear of the future. He was bankrupt. He had a cerebral hemorrhage that left him partially paralyzed. He worried that the creative spark that had made him rich was gone.

He was depressed. The texts that were his friends and that his soul could hear were texts such as "Why have you forsaken me?"

In the midst of his depression, a man came by who had compiled scriptures together in a semi-orderly fashion. He suggested that the songwriter put some music to the text. The writer looked at the text that read, "He was despised and rejected of humanity," and he felt that way, too. He read texts of the one for whom "no one had pity." He read about the one who trusted God still. He read the words, "I know that my redeemer liveth." He read the words "rejoice" and "hallelujah." That night George Frederic Handel was blessed by a "gentle cosmic light." He was led slowly out of darkness by a desire to write music at a feverish pitch. He worked tirelessly for days until, with manuscript complete, he dropped into a seventeen-hour, death-like sleep. A doctor was summoned to see if he was alive. Out of depression came the light of the *Messiah.* Out of that depression was left for us a light that would light the corridors of the lives of countless millions for all ages. Out of that darkness, a man in a deep depression began, as Stevenson said of the lamplighter, "punching holes in the darkness."

God punched holes in the darkness through Jesus. Jesus at the end of his life left us words that we can use as we anticipate the coming of the Christ. "Take heed. Listen. Be awake." "Your extremity is God's opportunity."

God is coming to make you new in this Advent season by interior design. Your job is to show up. God will do the rest. Peace to you as we together begin the long journey in darkness toward the marvelous light of Bethlehem. Amen.

Made New By Getting Lost

Advent 2   *Luke 3:1-6*

For those of you who have come here feeling lost, I have good news for you. For those of you who have come here willing to get lost, I have even better news. The good news is "fear not." The God we worship specializes in finding lost people. The God we worship gives life the moment we lose ours for the sake of heavenly causes.

Our text has two words that become backdrops for the entire season of Advent. Those words are "wilderness" and "about face." John comes out of the wilderness, the necessary passage on our pilgrimage toward God. Wilderness signifies being lost. We fear such moments, but God invites us to embrace those moments.

Michael Podesta was visiting our congregation recently along with his calligraphy work which inspires us in all seasons. One of his works has these words:

> *If as Herod, we fill our lives with things and again with things; if we consider ourselves so unimportant that we must fill every moment of our lives with action; when will we have time to make the long slow journey across the desert wilderness as did the Magi? Or sit and watch the stars as did the shepherds? Or brood over the coming of the child as did Mary? For each one of us there is a desert*

> *wilderness to travel; a star to discover; and a being within ourselves to bring to life.*

In coming to our congregation, Michael Podesta followed the wilderness path to our doorstep. Michael came here just two weeks after his teenage daughter was killed in a tragic car accident. When we heard this news, we told him we would understand if he needed to cancel his visit. He said we might not understand his need to come. He came here fresh from the wilderness of intense pain. He left us, blessed. There were moments when he told others what had happened. He was greeted by parents who shared the same tears. Parents who had loved and lost children of all ages embraced his life, and helped him to begin the long trek out of the wilderness toward the healing that will never be complete.

Hear this deep and often terrible truth: your being lost or getting lost in the desert wilderness is a clear sign of God's nearness. Turn around! God is near!

I. We get lost.

We get lost oftentimes on streets that were once familiar. I remember a man who told me about going back to his hometown where he knew no one. He said that it was a very different journey to go to one's hometown and stay in a hotel. The streets were familiar, but the faces were not.

When I go to my hometown in California, the growth has been so great since my leaving in 1961 that I get lost on streets that were once country roads but now have condominiums. I have joked for a long time about getting lost in my hometown. That town is especially different for me this Advent season. My father no longer lives there. I have never known that town without my father being alive to show me around those country roads with condos. This Advent is different.

We get lost with too many open doors. I learned long ago that children at play are most secure when there are boundaries and clearly marked limits to where they can go. They play in that designated space with confidence and with joy. If you place the same children in an open field and tell them they can play everywhere, you will find them huddling in the middle and playing in a small area. We get lost with too many options as children and as adults.

Hans Sach wrote a book titled *Masks of Love and Life*. In this novel there are two brothers. The younger one is afraid at night as they go to bed and always wants the bedroom door closed. The older brother doesn't care and is always upset when the younger one whimpers after going to bed that he wants the door closed. One night the older brother bolts out of the bed with rage. "Someday I'm going to lock you in a room with open doors," he says. And in that moment he describes our dilemma: we all quest after more options and don't know what to do when we get them. We are locked in by too many choices.

When I go to a computer store, they always tell me what I can do with a computer, including turning the heat on and off and doing my checking account on it. What they never seem to hear is this: all I want to do is write and have a good filing system for all I write. I will turn the heat on with my hand!

We get lost with too many open doors; too many options given.

We get lost with bad directions. Robert Fulghum spoke once of playing hide-and-seek. He says that some people get confused. The idea is to hide and get found, not to hide and never be found. He reflects:

> *As I write this, there is a kid under a pile of leaves in the yard just under my window. He has been there for a long time and everybody else is found and they are about to give up on him at the base. I consider finking on him or setting the leaves on fire to drive him out, but that's a bit radical. So I yelled, "Get found, kid" out the window and scared him so bad he wet his pants and started crying. It's hard to know how to be helpful sometimes.*

Sometimes adults hide too well. Many of us know someone who has died of cancer and never said a word to anyone. Friends share how brave he was and how he never complained. But after the memorial service, the family members come to their ministers in secret. They tell us how angry they are that the one they lost did not trust their strength, that he did not say good-bye. Adults often hide too well without knowing the importance of being found.

We get lost with our hands full. Thomas Moore has written an excellent book on spirituality titled *Meditations: On the Monk Who Dwells in Daily Life.* In the book he says:

> *Early Christian monks went out to live in the desert in order to find emptiness. Modern life is becoming so full that we need our own ways of going to the desert to be relieved of our plenty. Our heads are crammed with information, our lives busy with activities, our cities stuffed with automobiles, our imaginations bloated on pictures and images, our relationships heavy with advice, our jobs burdened with endless new skills, our homes cluttered with gadgets and conveniences. We honor productivity to such an extent that the unproductive person or days seem a failure. Monks are experts at doing nothing and tending the culture of that emptiness.*

Moore concludes by saying, *"At the sight of nothing, the soul rejoices!"*

I find that when I entertain this need to people, they absolutely shudder and protest, saying, "There is no time whatsoever for silence, emptiness, and reflection." There is no way around the need for the contemplative. How amazing it is to watch people embrace all of the noise that makes their life a mess, and still embrace the noise and expect different results from the chaos.

There was a little boy who was told he needed to pray in silence every day. He wrote a note to his minister saying, "I try to pray, Reverend. And I have this special place in my room where I keep the Bible open. But when I try to concentrate on Jesus, Michael Jordan keeps coming to mind."

I saw a T-shirt recently which read, "You are only young once, but you can be immature forever." And so can we spiritually.

Advent is the beginning of a time to grow up. The first step is getting lost in solitude and emptiness — the very places where God finds us.

II. We are found.

We are found when we stop distancing ourselves from pain. You will hear too many times from this pulpit that chaos is always created in the life of the one you seek to heal, convert, or fix. Parker Palmer identified a deeper distancing in which we cause great pain to one who suffers. He said:

> *Distancing ourselves from each other's pain is the hidden agenda behind most of our efforts to fix each other with advice. If you take my advice, and do it right, you will get well and I will be off the hook. But if you do not follow my advice, or do not follow it properly, I am off the hook nonetheless: I have done the best I could, and your continued suffering is clearly your fault. By trying to fix you with advice, rather than simply suffering with you, I hold myself away from your pain.*

We are found when we are open to holy disorder. Nancy Baker, editor of our church paper, is among the most well-read persons I know. She recalled a novel I spent time with by Morris West, titled *The Clowns of God*. In one place the main character lifts up how we all want order in our lives. He says that God comes in disorder, chaos, emptiness, and vulnerability.

> *This is why the coming of Jesus is a healing and saving event. He is not what we should have created for ourselves. His is truly the sign of peace, because He is the **sign of contradiction.** His career is a brief tragic failure. He dies in dishonor, but then, most strangely, he lives. He is not only yesterday. He is today and tomorrow. He is as available to the hum-blest as to the highest.*

We are found when we get a new perspective on the same thing. This is the holiest of gifts we receive in worship. That is what we do here: give new perspective to problems that have existed from the beginning.

Glenn Adsett was a minister in China. He was under house arrest in the late 1940s, waiting to receive word concerning what the communists were going to do with him, his wife, and two children. They said, "You can only take 200 pounds with you." The family went home and began arguing about what to take. The conversation got heated around typewriters, vases, and toys. Finally they worked it all out and packed 200 pounds on the nose. The army men came for them and asked if they were ready. "Yes, we are," they replied. "Did you weigh everything?" They answered affirmatively. Then the soldiers asked, "Did you weigh the kids?"

Suddenly there was an about-face: in that moment the typewriter and vase and books looked like trash in the shadow of their children's combined 200 pounds.

John the Baptist came from the emptiness of the desert and said, "Repent — about-face." That word was not one of judgment, but grace. The God we worship makes straight the paths of our lives and finds us in the midst of paradox, contradiction, chaos, disorder and emptiness.

So, in Advent, turn around. Get lost, that God might find you.

Fred Craddock reminds us of the way to get to Bethlehem. People of old got there by way of the wilderness. Today you can get to Bethlehem without going through the wilderness, *but when you get to Bethlehem,* Fred warns, *you will not find Jesus.*

May God grant us courage for the wilderness journey toward Bethlehem, that we might take the difficult, empty path. May God grant that we not be looking elsewhere as God comes to find us and give us the gifts of wonder, love, and grace. Amen.

Made New
By 180 Degrees

Advent 3 *Luke 3:7-18*
(and Philippians 4:4-9)

For those of you who have come here a mite tense today, I have good news for you. Without tension you cannot know the ultimate joy of Christmas. Without facing tension, Christmas is almost certainly missed.

We have a tension between our texts today. We find tension between what John says and what Paul proclaims in Philippians. Two things emerge from the texts.

First, the essential problem with John the Baptist. William Willimon, Chaplain at Duke University, says that John the Baptist reminds us of boundaries we must respect and gates we must pass through. At Duke, Willimon reminds the students, "If you are going to graduate, you must first get past the English Department. If you are going to practice law, you must pass the bar. If you want to get to medical school you must survive Organic Chemistry." Likewise, "If you want to get to the joy of Bethlehem in the presence of Jesus, you must get past John the Baptist in the desert." The word from John is "repent," which means "about-face" or turning 180 degrees.

Second, there is an essential message from Paul. Paul is basically saying that he wants us to be happy, not in a surface way, but in a deep way. He says that we can find that kind of happiness by doing the following: be tolerant of every person; worry about nothing; have peace that passes understanding; pray for things that you need, not that you want. We hear these words as simple pabulum and trite advice, until we recognize that Paul uttered these words in prison before a trial that could lead to his death. You want to talk about tension? With that tension in mind, read Paul's words again:

> *Rejoice!*
> — *Let your gentleness be known to everyone!*
> — *Do not worry about anything!*
> — *In everything by prayer and thanksgiving, let God know what you want!*
> — *And the peace of God which passes all understanding will guard your hearts and your minds in Christ Jesus!*

The kind of tension I have experienced at Christmas has nothing to do with the texts that are set before us, but the tasks that are set before me on Christmas Eve *after* the 11:00 service. When my children were small, that was when I would head home and get their presents wrapped and ready. The most horrifying experience was to open a box and find a slip that read "some assembly required." Well, that meant to someone like me, "You are going to be up all night and lose any religion you got from that Christmas Eve service." Or on other occasions, I would find the instructions at the bottom of the box after having put most of the toy together. My kids still laugh to this day about the tricycle I was assembling that turned out to be a small swing set.

The best story I have ever heard was about parents who got a treehouse to assemble for their kids, but it had instructions enclosed for a sailboat. Apparently the company caught their mistake and put a last minute disclosure on the box. The slip read: "While we regret the inconvenience the mistake must have caused you, it is nothing compared to that of the man who is out on a lake somewhere trying to sail your treehouse." The greatest stress of the season is often experienced just after the 11:00 service, especially when "some assembly is required."

The tension between these two biblical texts is felt also in the first Christmas card that was ever printed. It all started in 1843 with J.C. Horsley. He made a card that had a Victorian family at the dinner table. When opened, the inscription on the card read: "Feed the hungry; clothe the naked." His friends didn't like it. They thought it was rather "graphic and in poor taste." His friends were like most of us: we want the joy of Bethlehem without passing the hard reality being shouted by John.

Annie Dillard gives me help and hope. In her book *Pilgrim at Tinker Creek,* she said this: "I cannot cause light, the most I can do is try to put myself in the path of its beam." We cannot alleviate the tension that we feel; we can't really do a good job at changing what John says needs changing, and most of us cannot rejoice like Paul. The most we can do is allow ourselves to be made new, because we can't do it ourselves. We let ourselves be made new by 180 degrees — we learn to turn and look in the opposite direction at just the moment we cannot make things new in ourselves or right in the world. We pray that we might walk into the light rather than create it.

So what do we do? First, we **embrace tension**.

I remember the Great Flying Wallenda family. I remember a tragic accident that killed one of the family members and left two others severely injured. A reporter went to find the father of the family on the day after the accident. The reporter found the father practicing on the high wire. The reporter shouted for him to come down. In the interview the reporter pleaded, "What do you think you are doing? Your family member has been killed and you are out practicing the next day?" Wallenda replied quietly and with deep knowing, "To be on the wire is life. Everything else is simply waiting." He long ago responded to what he must do in life, and embraced the tension and made friends with it. And on that day when he was 72 years of age and fell off the high wire in Puerto Rico, I did not cry for him because I remembered his words that have stuck with me: "To be on the wire is life; all else is simply waiting."

I think it is time that we identify the person with the most stress in this season, and that is the Virgin Mary. We have her so wrapped up in serenity and halos that we cannot see the everyday misery that she was going through at the first Christmas.

Thomas Holmes made a stress scale, giving numbers to certain events that cause stress. The higher the number, the greater the stress. I will give you some of Holmes' numbers and my own numbers for Mary's stress level:

Calculated pregnancy	40 points
Unwanted pregnancy	20 points
Pregnant by Holy Spirit	30 points

(I'm going to give her 30 more points, because I can't imagine how she explained that to her mother.)

Change in living conditions   25 points

(Remember she went to live with Elizabeth and lived out of a suitcase. That is always stressful.)

Marriage to Joseph   50 points

(Any marriage brings this. Trying to explain her pregnancy to Joseph gets her another 25 points in my book.)

Change in financial status   38 points

(Joseph's work was erratic at best.)

No reservation at the inn   35 points

(You know how married couples argue over who should have done that.)

Birth	39 points
Change in sleeping habits	16 points
Change in eating habits	15 points
Uninvited guests; Magi came late and unannounced	50 points

(Includes shepherds and what they dragged in on their sandals. Also includes angels — how do you entertain them?)

Dr. Holmes says that people get sick with 200 stress points. Mary's ordeal earns her well over 400 points — an all-time high!

Now, let's get up and go home and repent of our griping for having too much stress in this season!

But, before you leave, remember what we have learned from the violinists. If the string is too tight, it breaks. If it is too loose, they can't make music. In this season and all seasons we are not trying to avoid stress, but we are looking for enough stress to make music, and enough tautness to be able to walk the wire of our uniqueness.

J. Walter Cross was flying a kite with his son Jay in Florida. The kite went very high and the pull of the string became greater. Finally, a storm came up and the winds blew harder and harder and the string finally broke. Cross said, "We are never free until we are restrained by something that pulls us higher." We know in time that lack of restraints and no stress does not make us free. The joy of heaven is known only when we are tethered to that which raises us: we turn toward pain and the difficult rather than run from them.

The last lesson we learn is to walk toward our own suffering or that of a friend. John Carmody was seriously ill. He presented an address which he titled "Theology of Illness." He spoke to clergy and theologian alike by saying:

> *When you deal with people seriously ill, either yourself or others, try to honor the eloquence of **God's silence**. Babble if you must ... but accept every invitation to desist. If the illness is your own, go for a walk, sit in a chapel, or just hold the loved ones you most cherish. If the illness is another's, listen for the time to hold silence — to take it to your bosom like a dove. There is a time to assault God, accuse God, but also a time to wait and leave God free ... **you did not make yourself, and you cannot raise yourself**. But what you cannot do, God can.*

A member of this congregation came to me recently and said, "The last lesson we learn in the church is the art of suffering silently with a friend without trying to fix them, isn't it?" She is right. The tension seems too great and so we babble. And God does come in deep ways still to those who face the tension of silence until that same silence becomes healing.

A wonderful man in San Diego came to me once and told me about his father's premature death. I told him that no matter what age our fathers are when they die, their death for us is always premature.

He said, "Now don't give me any of your theologian stuff or things you've read from seminary books. Tell me the bottom line from your experience about how we get over this awful chapter of life."

I shot from the hip and replied:
1. Nothing anyone says will help you or make your pain subside. Friends intend well with words, and words don't help.
2. No book you will be given will do you any good.
3. Only time will heal in ways you can't explain.
4. I can't give you anything but myself, and a willingness to sit in silence with you. I will let you say whatever you want and I will allow you to say nothing if need be.

When we embrace the tension that is inherent in silent suffering, God visits us as surely as God dropped into Bethlehem.

A second thing we do after embracing tension is to **pay attention**.

Someone has suggested that we pay attention to the contemplated expressions of the season — that includes paintings by Raphael and a glance at the Sistine Chapel, a modern translation of the Psalms, or to remember that Handel wrote the *Messiah* out of a deep depression and despair that he faced with open hands. Contemplated expressions of the season help us pay attention to the most important things at Advent.

And then, we need to pay attention more to the spontaneous expressions of the season. I remember the story of a boy who had a hard time in school. They said he was "slow." He was well-liked and loved at both school and church. At church they wanted to include him in the Christmas pageant, so they carefully arranged to have him play a part with just one line. He was the innkeeper.

He was to say one line only: "I'm sorry but there is no room in the inn." That's it. No big deal.

When it came time for him to say his line, as he opened the door and saw Joseph and Mary standing there, he said, "I know what I am supposed to say, but Mary! Joe! Come on in — you can have my room!" He didn't get the line right, but he got the deepest meaning of this season in his spontaneous response in the presence of the holy.

When I was senior minister in San Diego, our Early Childhood Development program started growing rapidly. More room was needed. During the remodeling process, some of the children would be playing right outside my office window. It was decided to soundproof my wall for the sake of quiet, and construction began. As construction progressed, I could hear the final greeting of every mother and father to their child as they were dropped off. I remember one mother's voice that almost convinced me not to soundproof. She said, "Jimmy, remember I love you forever and always. I will see you tonight and I will not be late. Mommy and Daddy love you very much. Bye!" It spontaneously dawned on me: if every child were to hear those magic words enough until they were ten years of age, eighty percent of the counseling needs of this country would disappear in the years ahead.

Was it a frustrated God who in one spontaneous God moment chose a manger to send that same greeting to us? "I'll love you forever and always — my adored child you shall forever be!" The story of this season must be true, for only God could think up such a spontaneous move on the human family.

Vicky always spoke spontaneously to me. Very old, she would greet me at the door of the church and I would brace myself for what she would say. Often she would say, "I loved your sermon — last Sunday!" That left me dangling and wondering how badly I had blown it just moments previously, but I could also see the twinkle in her eye and the delight in keeping at least one clergy humbled. No easy task.

One year during Advent I went to see Vicky for what we all knew were her last days on earth. I came to her during a time in my life that was not good at all. I didn't want to be in a convalescent home and it must have shown. In a clergy hurry, I entered her room. I stood there for a moment and she took my hand. She looked me straight in the eye and said, "Waiting is hard for you, isn't it?" Her spontaneous words that I believe came straight from God left me crying uncontrollably. Then with the smile of an angel, she looked at me and said, "You know what I am waiting for, don't you?" In three days, we gathered to give thanks to God for her life that now had disappeared from us.

Vicky made me see Milton, the poet, sitting in his blindness, saying, "They also serve who only sit and wait." Vicky helped me to understand that the greatest moments of life will not be in the things that we arrogantly believe we must make happen, but will be in those moments that we allow God to give us what God knows we need. I shall never forget Vicky's faith.

So, we have come here in tension, and have been greeted by more tension. We sit with the tension between the awful demands of John in the desert that we "turn around" and look another direction and face what we must face. Then we look to the imprisoned Paul who says:

> *Rejoice!*
> — *Let your gentleness be known to everyone!*
> — *Do not worry about anything!*
> — *In everything by prayer and thanksgiving, let God know what you want!*
> — *And the peace which passes all understanding, will guard your hearts and your minds in Christ Jesus!*

We immediately feel like the moment Woody Allen described. He said, "We stand before two paths. One of them leads to destruction; the other to total despair. May God help us to choose the right one!" It feels like a choice between John's gruffness in the desert and Paul's joy in prison are not options between which we would like to choose.

Somehow, we realize that the joy of which Paul speaks is on the other side of facing the tension and anxiety that underlies human life: to realize that the only way around it is through it. And in facing that tension, we realize that we have walked gently into a beam of light that no life seeking leisure can know. That light is from Bethlehem. That light is just as available to us right now as it was to shepherds long ago.

May God help us to receive the gift of that light which gives life. Amen.

Made New
By Taking A Different Road Home

Advent 4 *Luke 1:39-45*
(and Micah 5:2-51; Hebrews 10:5-10)

We are made new when we dare to go home by another way. This reality has ancient roots. The stories of the season are about people who were made new by taking a different road home.

Mary visited Elizabeth and remained there three months. She went home by another way. After saying earlier, "Do with me as you will," before God, and after singing her song of praise to God, she went home a different way.

Bethlehem is a place from which, once you've been there, you cannot go home the same way. The shepherds may have taken the same road there, but the way home was different. The Magi were warned in a dream to "leave by another route." Joseph and Mary would be warned also in a dream to head to Egypt by a circuitous route. The road *to* Bethlehem and the road *from* Bethlehem are never the same. You can't bow at the manger and see the world the same again.

Poets know this. Robert Frost would poetically inform us that "here is before each of us a decision, much like a fork in the road. Having been where we have been, having seen what we have seen, we must now decide who we will be." The poets know about the roads that lead us to places that never leave us the same.

Another poet reflected on the Magi searching for truth and finding their way to Bethlehem. When asked how far they will go for the truth, one Magi responded by saying, "Not too far, just far enough so we can say we've been there." Is that us? We will be hanging around the manger for several weeks in this season. The question we must ask is how far down a different path we will let this little town take us.

Several angles of vision stand before us as we think of the road to and the road from Bethlehem.

The road to Bethlehem is hurried; the road from Bethlehem has speed bumps. The most laughable moments in this season surround people who are in too much of a hurry. For me, the most laughable moment in this season was my trip to the Post Office fourteen days before Christmas. I must let you know that the best invention of the postal service has been those peel-off stamps. Since my wife used to give me the job of licking stamps at Christmas, I see that as a modern miracle. Posted on the door of the Post Office, a sign read, "We are all out of peel-off Christmas stamps. We still have Christmas stamps that must be moistened to affix." That seemed clear enough to me. A woman stepped up to the counter and insisted on getting the peel-off ones. The kind man informed her that they were all out, but that he had the ones that needed moistening. She went into a tirade about the postal service and the man listened. Finally, she said she would take the ones that needed moistening, and when they were handed to her, she told the postal worker that HE needed to lick them and put them on her cards because she was too busy and in a hurry. At that, the whole line of people broke out laughing. The kind man simply gave her a complaint card to fill out that could be sent to his supervisor.

I also read about a lady who was hurrying to get her cards out in the mail. She noticed some Christmas cards already on sale before Christmas and swooped up dozens of them. She mailed them out without reading the greeting. To her horror, she read after mailing them that the greeting was: "This card is just a note to say, a little gift is on the way!"

Three men were running through an airport in San Diego and knocked down the small apple stand that was being run by a boy in tattered clothes. Two men kept running to meet the plane and the third had the good sense to stop, help the boy stack the apples, buy two of them and leave him a nice tip. The boy looked at the face of this man who took the time to help and asked, "Are you Jesus?" The road to Bethlehem is hurried. The road from Bethlehem is slower and looks at faces instead of clocks. Those who take the different way home look divine. They are the ones who take time for things that have ultimate importance.

A boy in the first grade was asked, "What is a grandparent?" He answered, "Someone with time."

The road from Bethlehem reveals the sliver of the divine that is in all of us. Dr. F. Forrester Church, a Unitarian minister, said that "we can't see the divine in ourselves easily, so we have to recognize it in others." The gift of Jesus, he said, was this: "When we gazed into his eyes, we would see divine eyes, and we would see our own eyes. When we saw his tears, we would recognize our own. And when we saw the elegance of his actions, and the simplicity of his teachings, and the essence of his loving-kindness, we would recognize our own. And then we would be changed — *into that which we already were but had lost sight of until it was revealed to us!*"

The best gift of this season could be the reminder that God has intended to give the world a gift through the uniqueness of your personality. The world is robbed of something precious and unique if you don't give your gift. Meister Eckhardt said, "Become aware of what is in you. Announce it, pronounce it, produce it, and give birth to it."

The road from Bethlehem reveals strength in weakness. Dr. Cornish Rogers is a teacher at the School of Theology in Claremont, California. I attended a spiritual life retreat that he conducted and found him to be a wonderful mentor of spiritual discipline. Not until long after that retreat did I find a new appreciation for his depth and his gift.

Dr. Rogers' son, David, is weak. At 29 years of age, a star graduate of Harvard Medical School, David came home for the holidays. While driving along a freeway in southern California, a tire flew off a semi-truck, bounced on top of David's car, and left him a paraplegic.

There is another David in this story. His name is David Kaplan. He was born mentally handicapped. He lived in a sheltered environment for fourteen years and developed skills for independent living. Two weak Davids got together to slay the giant of genetics and accident and work hand in hand together. David Rogers went on with his medical career thanks to David Kaplan. "David Kaplan is my hands. He does everything for me, from delivering and getting records to making phone calls ... He remembers the phone numbers of people I saw or spoke to months ago. He's invaluable." Two men taking weakness and turning it into a strength that medically serves hundreds of people.

The road from Bethlehem reveals strength within weakness.

The road to Bethlehem is harmless; the road from Bethlehem is explosive. A Roman Catholic priest was entering Israel with a group of nuns and lay people who were on a spiritual pilgrimage. If you have been there you know that there are soldiers everywhere and that they carry guns and have been on constant alert since the nation began in the late 1940s. The security guards at the airport brought out dogs to sniff for explosives. One dog centered in on a nun and spent an inordinate amount of time checking her out. It seems that she had some food in her purse. The guards were a little embarrassed. They said, "We must make sure there is nothing explosive here."

That's what we do with Bethlehem. We sniff it out and defuse it. We make sure there is nothing explosive there. And in fact, at Bethlehem we were entrusted with the most explosive message ever. The message is: "You can't earn God's love because God chooses to give it to us." The message of the manger is as explosive as a simple reading of Matthew 5 or Galatians 5 where we are told "for freedom Christ has set you free; never go back to slavery again." Yet, the Church has worked hard throughout history to take that which is given freely and put a toll gate in front of it. And yet the gospel goes off like a bomb to anyone who will appeal directly to that word of Good News.

How is the message diffused? How does such power become pabulum? A bishop asked that dangerous question to an actor once. The bishop inquired, "Why is it that we preachers usually make little impression with the lofty and true subjects that we proclaim, while you actors move people on the stage so much with your fiction?" The actor replied, "It is because we speak of fictitious things as though they were true, whereas the clergy talk about true things as though they were fictitious."

Something is explosive about Advent. Four weeks ago a fuse was lit and we have been waiting for detonation to occur. The story doesn't come through carved figures on a mantel. The story happens through flesh and blood — God incarnate — your Christ comes!

All this happens from taking a different road home. James Taylor wrote a popular and intriguing song about the Magi. The song is titled "Home By Another Way." In part it reads:

> *Those magic men the Magi ...*
> *They went home by another way*
> *Maybe we can be wise too ...*
> *And go home by another way*

May we in this season go "home by another way," that we might be found by the One who is the way, the truth, and the life. Amen.

Yours For The Asking

Christmas Eve/Day *Luke 2:1-20*

I would like to invite you to do the most difficult thing that can be asked of our culture, and that is to do nothing. I invite you to approach this night with open hands and hearts and do nothing. This night is not about effort, but about receiving. This night's gift is yours for the asking and without effort.

While in the Atlanta airport a friend of mine went into a restaurant where he was served something he had never seen before. He inquired, "What is this white glob here on the plate?" The waitress said, "Those are grits." "But I didn't order grits," he said, while looking at the check. She finally said, "You don't order grits. They just come!" And you don't order Advent. You don't order grace. You don't order God. God comes on God's time and in God's way, not ours.

I was on my way to visit a woman who was in the hospital one December and received instructions in a very unlikely place. I drove up to one of those single-board barriers that stand at the exit to a parking lot. I got close enough to see the words on the wooden sign. It read, "Approach the gate slowly, and it will open." Good advice for Bethlehem. Approach it slowly and God will open to you all that you need.

Three things are needed without effort this night.

I. Look up.

There was a boy who had watched his father put up a lighted sign on top of the house for years. When he became ten years of age, his father told him to put the sign up for Christmas. The boy was proud to do it in record time and plugged it in. He went in the house bursting with pride, but the neighbors were rolling with laughter. He spelled "Noel" backward. In flashing lights it read "Leon" on top of the house.

Perhaps he was on to something. We don't know people named Noel, but we all know someone named Leon. Leon, his friend, knew Christmas was special because his friend Joe put his name on the roof. Leon is lucky because God does come to us through the power of the personal on this night.

On this night God comes in a holy child by the power of the personal. God comes with your names on the lips of the holy one of Bethlehem. God comes not to reprimand, but to remind you of the love God holds for you forever.

Look up! God comes by the power of the personal.

II. Enjoy the chaos.

I think it is time for us to enjoy the chaos of the season. I went to City Center this last week with a quick list and found that you don't do anything quickly at a shopping mall in December. I talked to a colleague at the beginning of the season who said, "It's terribly hectic and crazy. I love every minute of it!"

We go to a lot of trouble in this season, and that trouble has a note of triumph about it. There was a Catholic nun who was leaving a community in Africa where she had served for over ten years. As she was leaving, a young man came up to her and said, "I have a gift." He gave her a seashell. She adored it and thanked him. "Where did you get it?" she asked. He told her that he had gone to the ocean and got it. "That is a hundred miles away. How did you get there?" He said he walked. "Why did you go to this trouble?" she shyly asked. He said, "The trouble is part of the gift." And so is our willingness to go through the effort, chaos, and pain to say to others that we care. God has constantly created good out of chaos and we pray that God will do the same with the healthy and unhealthy chaos we bring to this season.

And finally,

III. Ask for more.

Yes, you heard me correctly: ask for more.

In my family they always knew Christmas was near, because I would get sick. I got so excited about getting things that I would run a fever and end up in bed. My family didn't need one of those Advent calendars where you open one little box each day of the month. They had me! "Dick's getting sick. Christmas is near!" My father was worried about my greed. He told me once that it was "more blessed to give than to receive." I told him that I would bless many people by allowing them to give me things. He insisted that I missed the point.

There was a famous golfer from our country who went to Saudi Arabia to teach the king how to play golf. The king had over thirty golf courses and no one, including himself, played too well. So, for a large sum of money, one of our famous golfers gave him golf lessons. Weeks went by and it was time for the golfer to leave. An emissary for the king came to him and said, "The king would like to know what gift you would like upon leaving." The golfer said he had been paid well and didn't need anything. The emissary insisted and told the golfer that he would offend the king by not naming a gift. Finally the golfer said, "Just tell him to give me a golf club. That will be fine."

The next day the emissary came and announced that the king was delighted with the request. Then the golfer was presented with a golf club. He was handed *the deed to an eighteen-hole golf course!* And the moral of the story is this: in the presence of the king, ask for no small gifts.

In the presence of the king this night remember to look up. God comes repeating your name with love. Enjoy the chaos, for God creates best in chaos. Ask for more, for God wants you to have more than what you ask; God wants you to have what you need. Then with open hands you will find that "all your hope and all your fears" of all your years will be met in this child this night.

Let us pray:

> God, we are as confounded as Joseph and Mary, as busy as the innkeepers, as lonely as the shepherds, as frightened as Herod, as wayfaring as the Magi. Turn us again to the place where, with quietness, you wrap up your truth and promise, your love and salvation in the Child born in a rude barn. We ponder these things as the noise and clamor of the world is stilled for a time and there is a peace that settles deep within us. Bring us to Bethlehem, to the place where Jesus was homeless but where we are truly at home. Amen.

Living By The Calendar Instead Of The Clock

Christmas 1 *Luke 2:41-52*

This is the time of year that we look toward 1998 with new resolve, or observe how far we have wandered from last year's resolutions. Have you ever noticed that New Year's resolutions look strangely familiar? As a matter of fact, don't they most often look exactly like last year's resolutions?

Too often in this season we look at the resolutions we made for our lives that we never got started. I was in a spiritual life retreat once with a group of clergy who were talking about the joys and pains of parish life. One dignified Roman priest told us that he was going on the fiftieth year of his ordination, which all of us applauded and celebrated. Within an hour this good priest was in tears. When he could finally speak he said, "Matthew 5. Matthew 5. Look how far all of us have wandered away from Matthew 5, those fiery words that attracted us to ministry in the first place." He had awakened to how far his call to ministry had been buried under the need to make budgets and committees work in parish life. Looking at failed resolutions that failed can be sad.

Looking at life resolutions can be a glad occasion. Robert Frost wrote poetry which rang a bell with many paths we have all taken, especially when he spoke of taking the "road less traveled" which has "made all the difference." How glad is the moment when we recognize that we followed the dictates of our hearts rather than those of a parent or other who had plans for our lives that did not fit our souls.

Too often we get too far away from the source that gives us life, fuels our spirit, and reveals our soul. We wander and forget. That is why we come here for worship. To remember what is important and to rediscover the lines we drew for ourselves in the past. I read the story about a man who painted lines in the middle of the road in the days when they did it by hand. He was entered in a contest. The first day he painted five miles of line, which was a new world record. The next day he painted only 500 feet. The next day just 27 feet. Someone asked why. The painter replied, "I kept getting farther and farther away from the bucket." We wander too far from the very source that gives us life and fuels our very being. We wander too far from the things that are most important.

The biblical story before us is of Jesus wandering too far away from his parents and getting a good chewing out, which, in my opinion, was warranted. A surface reading of the text is about a disobedient child. His mother said, in essence, "Child, why have you treated us like this? Look, your father and I have been searching for you in great anxiety." Jesus replies, "Why were you searching for me? Did you not know that I must be in my Father's house?" From the tranquility of the stable, Joseph and Mary are confronted by a pre-adolescent child who is making perplexing statements. Having a holy child is not all roses.

A deeper reading of the text would lead elsewhere. What does it mean to be in God's house? Jesus in time would give us an example of what that means. Jesus would not give a prescription, but an example. To be in God's house means living by the calendar instead of the clock. The life of Jesus would invite us to live our lives by keeping our eyes firmly fixed on ultimate concerns rather than passing fancy. He calls us to live by the calendar of faith rather than the clock of fads. He invites us to live fixed on the importance of persons above possessions. He invites us to live in the theatre with a large screen, not in the daily snapshots that are trimmed to fit our wallets.

The wider witness of Jesus invites us to live several ways.

I. Jesus invites us to leisure.

How many times did Jesus say to his disciples, "Let us go off by ourselves to some place where we will be alone and can rest awhile?" How many times do we read, "So they went away in a boat to a deserted place by themselves?" Have we ever entertained the notion that perhaps Jesus set the best example for our lives when he went away often to be alone and contemplate on that which was most important?

When I was in seminary in the late 1960s, a question was posed to us: Because we are entering the computer age that will take care of the problems we normally spend time with, what will we, as clergy, do to help the people in our congregation with their leisure time? Can you believe that? How can we miss future predictions by that wide a margin? Instead, we know that with every problem we solve, we create two more problems, all of which demand our time. We know now that more than any other time in history the chief complaint in family and individual life is that "there is no time."

"Leisure," from the Latin, means "to be free." *Leisure is anything that restores you to peace while you are doing it.* So, gardening, golf, reading, puzzles, and many other things can restore us to peace as we do them. Another cousin of leisure is the word "parargon." This little-used word means "the second thing that we do in life that keeps the first thing in tune." Hence, our work may draw energy from us, and we have then a "parargon," a leisure thing we do in order to restore us.

Most often, to build toward leisure demands that we disassemble something else. In Thomas Moore's book *Meditations,* he tells of a pilgrim walking along a road. The pilgrim sees some men working on a stone building.

"You look like a monk," the pilgrim said.
"I am that," said the monk.
"Who is that working on the abbey?"
"My monks. I'm the abbot."
"It's good to see a monastery going up," said the pilgrim.
"They're tearing it down," said the abbot.
"Whatever for?" asked the pilgrim.

"So we can see the sun rise at dawn," said the abbot.

My church will be called to build in three places this next year, and we will succeed in doing that. However, we must make sure that all our building stays out of the path of the sun that shines on the face of one born in a manger, born to set us free! May God give us courage to remove anything from our lives that will keep us from seeing the face of the child of Bethlehem who leads us to live by the big picture instead of the small obstacles in life. Otherwise, all our building is in vain.

II. Jesus invites us to let him be the Messiah, not us.

There are people who would have more balance in their lives if they did not accept responsibility for everything that happens in the world.

We are buried in "oughts and shoulds" to such a degree that we feel responsible for everything that goes wrong in Columbus as well as in Calcutta. I have heard about a Catholic nun who had a little sign in her office that read, "Today I will not should on myself." We need to read it daily with her.

Terry Hershey has a note on a mirror in his bathroom which reads, "Dear Terry, I know being in control makes you feel better, but I can handle it. Thanks anyway. Love, God.

A popular coffee mug says, "Who nominated you Messiah today?"

How hard it is for us to hear the hymn, "When the wrong seems oft so strong, God is the ruler yet." Only living by the calendar instead of the clock will reveal this. Courage is needed for the kind of life that will trust things to God's time rather than our limited schedule.

III. Jesus invites us to exercise the spirit as well as the mind and body.

I read the words of Dr. Meyer Friedman, who said that lifestyle and creative use of leisure can be more important than diet and exercise in preventing heart attacks. Obviously a balance among all three is most desirable. I have observed many people who have paid attention to the body and diet and have neglected the spirit and are dying inside.

Dr. Friedman gives suggestions for people to live less frantic lives by living more by the calendar than the clock:
1. Stop thinking about several things at one time.
2. Listen without interrupting.
3. Read books that demand concentration (games, too).
4. Avoid irritating people.
5. Plan for some personal quiet time each day.
6. Finally, *things worth being are better than things worth having.*

Remember the people who were here first. The Native Americans had an ability to live by the ages rather than by the day. Among certain tribes in North America were those who would make decisions for the tribe based on *how that decision would affect people seven generations into the future!*

Parish ministers will tell you that people come to them speaking with regrets like these:

> *When I was young, my mother was going to read me a story, but she had to wax the bathroom floor and there wasn't time.*

> *When I was young, my grandparents were going to come for Christmas, but they couldn't get someone to feed the dogs and my grandfather did not like the cold weather and besides they didn't have time.*

> *When I was young, my father was going to listen to me read my essay on "What I Want To Be When I Grow Up," but there was Monday Night Football and there wasn't time.*

> *When I was young, my father and I were going to go hiking in the Sierras, but at the last minute he had to fertilize the lawn and there wasn't time.*

> *When I grew up and left home to be married, I was going to sit down with Mom and Dad and tell them I love them and would miss them, but my best man was honking the horn in front of my house so there wasn't time.*[1]

Into our hectic world, Jesus comes, and still invites us to exercise the spirit as well as the mind and the body. The best way we exercise the spirit is by giving attention to things of eternal significance, such as listening, loving, and learning from the least expected places.

IV. Jesus invites us to ordinary time.

It took me a long while to hear this truth from Mother Teresa: "There are no big deals anymore, just small things to be done with great love."

Most of this coming year will be spent in ordinary time. We enter into the season on the church calendar marked as "ordinary time." What a good prophetic note for the new year: most of the good that will be done will be done in ordinary time, when no one is looking and no one will report it to the paper.

Here comes the new year, full of ordinary time. We will enter it ready to slug it out for the common good while no one is looking. In the middle of ordinary time, God comes with extraordinary moments that make all others bearable, believable, and worthwhile.

I have always thought that while our nation works out negotiations with other countries, like with North Korea, we only see the leaders in the news. But, if the whole story were revealed, we would see nameless people on both sides of the issue tirelessly speaking to each other through the night in order to work out an agreement. Leaders sit down and sign documents that were slugged out by unknowns in the night during ordinary time.

Ordinary time reveals solutions right under our noses that demand the calendar instead of the clock. Each morning at 6:00 a.m. I read the abbreviated version of the *New York Times*. They were running an extensive overview of youth in trouble, their cases, and the solutions that worked. I was intrigued by one woman who has worked with youth in trouble for over twenty years. She said that she is aware of a solution that has worked 100 percent of the time. When a young person is taken from juvenile hall and assigned an adult mentor who will meet with the young person daily to talk with him or her, she never finds that young person returning to juvenile hall. We wring our hands and seek solutions by the clock and build more prisons, when all along the direction of a solution lies with the calendar: youth who will be given daily attention by an adult.

I have a friend who, when found by a youth minister, was in a drug stupor, lying on a park bench in a small Illinois town in the late 1960s. The youth minister was trying to help young people with drug problems. He came to the park and sat on the bench with this young man. He didn't try to convert him, but asked for his help. "I know you are on drugs. I am trying to help young people on drugs and I have a movie that I want to show them, but I need to know if the theme of the movie rings true. I myself have never been on drugs. Would you come and look at the movie and tell me if it is a good one to show to the youth?" The boy on the park bench followed the youth minister to church and saw the film. He volunteered to be the projectionist. That runaway boy found a home in a youth group and a reason to be off drugs. That boy became in time one of three of the best youth ministers I have ever met in my life. I remember working with him and observing the intense patience that he gave to every young person who came to him. He gave them himself. He gave them his time.

That boy on the bench turned out to be one of the best influences on my own children and hundreds of others. That boy on the bench has become a computer expert with such ability that he was the person who went to South Africa and ran the elections that moved Mandela to the presidency.

Thank God for a youth minister in Illinois who did not try to heal, convert, or fix my friend Mike Yard, but invited him by the calendar to a new way of life.

V. Jesus heals us in ordinary time.

The human family has a hidden desire for one special event in life to clear up a problem or a pain that it carries. Seldom if ever is there a word or event that heals our pain. In time we learn that pain is healed at a moment when we are not looking.

In the last century there was a man named Louie who was an expert at creweling leather. His designs were famous. One day while sharpening his tools, both eyes were blinded by flying pieces of steel from his disintegrated tools. Many weeks later he entered his workshop, newly blind, and angry. He felt the tools he would never use again and the leather with images he would never release. He started stabbing the leather in rage. His tears and anger were overdue. Without knowing it he stabbed a piece of paper. In time at that same desk he would learn that on the other side of the paper were little bumps. He learned that he could arrange the bumps in sequence. It was at that desk that Louie, Louie Braille, learned to lead thousands of people, including himself, out of darkness into light.

Later he would conclude that while looking at his blindness by a different angle of vision that he was healed. He was healed when his tragedy was turned into service for others that were blind like himself. It was in an extraordinary accident that he was blinded. It was in an ordinary moment in time that he discovered what could lead him and others to new light and life.

In December it is announced to all of us that the shortest day of the year has arrived. On that day there will be a minimum of light and a maximum of darkness. Often that day is clouded so that what light there is will not be seen. On that dark day I buried a woman in our church. I knew the day was dark for all, and I knew it was especially dark for this family to bury one they loved.

Deep in December we are asked to remember. We are asked to remember that with every day we face the dark, we will move minute by minute toward the brighter days of summer. And then, without realizing it, there will be more light than dark. All this happens when we are not looking. All this happens in ordinary time.

God comes to us, loves us, and finally heals us, not by the hourly watching of the clock, but by the monthly glance at the calendar. It is only by the calendar that we can hear these words:

> *Deep in December it's nice to remember*
> *Without a hurt the heart is hollow ...*
> *Deep in December our hearts will remember*
> *— and follow.*

Follow the star that leads to ordinary time and extraordinary love which we have seen and heard in Jesus Christ. Amen.

---

1. "Generating Good Signs" by Robert Capen, Jr., *Vital Speeches,* Aug. 1980.

Kneeling And Redirection

Epiphany   *Matthew 2:1-12*

Three wise men come from the east bringing gifts to the infant Jesus, and in the process receive a gift worth the distance and effort they spent. After depositing their gifts of gold, frankincense, and myrrh, they in turn receive a gift: **They are redirected.**

That is what we all get after kneeling before Jesus: we are redirected. That different direction after kneeling before Jesus means that *your joy in life will not be in seeking happiness and fulfillment directly, but in intentionally walking the way of service, sacrifice, and surrender.*

The new direction involves finding the holy in the least expected places, the very places we would most like to avoid.

I. Different Way Of Pain

Jesus redirects us by inviting us to face pain head-on rather than avoiding it, which is the way most people confront uncomfortability and pain.

I remember that moment in which Peter makes the great confession that Jesus is the Christ of God. Right after that Jesus says he will be opposed by the religious leaders and will be killed. That is when Peter takes Jesus aside and "rebukes him" (a strong Biblical word). In turn, Jesus rebukes Peter and says in essence, "Your refusal to face pain is the kind of work that is at its core evil."

Jesus then sets his face toward Jerusalem and faces the inevitable pain of life.

Jesus instructs us that our joy in life will not be in the escaping of pain and evil, but will be in the very midst of the storm of pain and evil. You might remember also that Peter was the one who protested that storm on the sea. When we read the words of Jesus, "Peace, be still," we make a grave error. We assume that he was talking to the weather, but he was not. He spoke to Peter. God does not come and take us away from the inevitable storms of life. God comes in the form of the promised presence of calm in the midst of whatever happens to us. God has never promised to take us away from any of life's disasters or pain. God has always promised to go *with us* through all of them. That promised presence makes the difference.

When we make friends with the fact that to live is to know pain and that it is better faced than escaped (which is never successful), then we can see more clearly. We can see that the common thread in the human family is the experience of pain. We are not united by joys. Joys are so varied, and people are joyous for very different reasons. We are not united by color or language or belief. We are united by those things that grieve us.

Carlisle Marney said, "All our grief comes from one thing: something ends before we were ready for it to end." I have never found a more common thread among people in parish life than in the conversations that I have had with people who lost their fathers like I did. The language of our pain and losses is the same.

Garrison Keillor told the story of the time that his mother and father took him to the city to visit an aunt who was lonely and alone after the death of her husband of 55 years. He describes how she looked to him at ten years of age. Her dress was stained with food spots, her rouge was heavy on one side, her lipstick was crooked, her fake pearls did not go with her dress. She sat at the table as they ate together. The aunt began to cry. "I have nothing left to live for. I might as well die." She started to cry as she kept chewing her food. "I'll bet that if I died tomorrow, no one would even come to my funeral, not even you folks." Garrison, seeking to be helpful at ten years of age, said, "Oh, I'd come. I'd be glad to come to your funeral." Reflecting on her outburst, Keillor concludes as he thinks back forty years: "Every tear that poor woman cried, we will cry also before we leave this world and give in to the one death we owe."

A rabbinical student came to love one of his teachers so much that he finally told the rabbi, "I love you, Rabbi!" The reply was swift. "How can you love me unless you know what hurts me?" We find in time that to know truly and be bound to one another is to be open to and share what hurts the other.

Jesus invites us toward Jerusalem to face pain rather than run from it. It is the only way we can get home, and the way we would most like to avoid.

II. Different Way Of Small Victories

On this day of Epiphany, which celebrates the light of Christ being spread into the world, it is a good time for us to make friends with the small victories that will be ours, rather than continue the myth that there are big deals that we must negotiate.

On this day, it is good for us to take a Mother Teresa 101 course. Three things she said will help us.

The first has to do with the time she came to her Bishop and asked that he create an order for her to lead that would take care of dying people on the streets. He asked her how much money she had. She pulled out two cents. He said that she could not build an order on two cents. She said, "With God and two cents you can do anything." She won a small victory of permission in order to paint her vision of much love for a dying world.

The second thing has to do with what Mother Teresa said just after she won the Nobel Peace Prize. She announced to the world: "There are no big deals anymore. Only many small things to be done with great love."

The third thing that Mother Teresa said that helps us in downward mobility in order to serve the Christ was this: "Don't think that by your little acts of kindness that you are going to change the world. AND it is so important that you do them."

Loren Eiseley comes running after the spirit of Mother Teresa in his description of the star-thrower. The star-thrower knows the power of small victories. The star-thrower is the man on the beach who is faced by millions of starfish washed ashore that will die in the day if they are not thrown back in. A man at breakfast watches from a distance as another man carefully throws some back, one at a time. He walks to the beach to talk to the star-thrower and asks him what he is doing. The reply dwells on the obvious. "I am throwing the starfish back in so they can live." The observer musters up some cynicism and says, "You don't think this will make a difference, do you?" The star-thrower holds up one starfish and says, "It makes a difference to this one." And he throws it in the ocean.

When Jesus asked us to let our light shine before all people, I am sure he did not have a lighthouse in mind, but simple everyday acts of kindness to be done in his name, most of which are given anonymously.

When I lived in San Diego, I was most impressed by the stories of two women who knew the meaning of small victories. Both lived in poor communities and wanted to make a contribution but didn't know what to do. The first lady had a vision of helping the kids in the neighborhood. She said the vision that came to her was God instructing her to back her car out of the garage. She did. Next she decided that the open room in the garage could be made into a place to teach and nurture the neighborhood children. She invited them in, taught them about God and self-esteem, and nurtured their reading and writing abilities. Many years later those young people come back from leading successful lives and proclaim that the difference was in this wonderful woman who backed her car out of the garage and gave her love to kids who needed it.

The other woman not far away wanted to feed the homeless in the neighborhood and could not get a permit from the city. Watching the people needing food daily, she decided to go the way of the Nike slogan and "Just Do It." The city said she could not feed people out of the front of the house, so she set up benches in the backyard and fed 150 people a day. When the city called, she said that it was not breaking the law: "These people are not homeless people or clients; they are my family. I always feed my family in the backyard of my home." And the city left her alone. She knew the different way that Jesus calls, the way of small victories done quietly in his name.

Someone said, "Life is what happens to you when you make other plans." Jesus says that life begins by taking a different way home than the world teaches. Jesus shows us that by kneeling in front of the divine, we get a new direction. That new direction includes facing the inevitable pain in life and developing a theology of small victories as we give ourselves to what God needs done next.

The way of Jesus is a longer way than we anticipated traveling and is most often on a road that we would not have chosen had we known where it was going. And the end of the journey is to discover that the redirected way of life that Jesus calls us to is, in fact, in miles and in blessing.

To walk the way of Jesus is to kneel before the holy with empty hands, not with the words "give me," but with the humble prayer that begins, "make me." At that moment Christ sets us on paths we would never have chosen. At the end of life, we discover that his redirected paths are the ones we would have chosen in the first place, had we known. Had we known that the human family is blessed by facing pain rather than running from it, and had we known that the deepest joy of all is in the small shafts of light we can shed on a suffering world, we would have gladly chosen the way of the Christ in the first place. Amen.

Echoes

Baptism Of The Lord 　　　　　　　　　*Luke 3:15-17, 21-22*

When I stand before this text, I hear an echo. What stands out most is the word from heaven as Jesus comes up from the water: "This is my son, the beloved. Listen to him." At another place in scripture where Jesus goes to the mountain with Peter, James, and John to "reveal" himself more pointedly in what we call the transfiguration, suddenly we hear the words of his baptism echo from heaven again: "This is my son, the beloved. Listen to him."

The echoes that reverberate from baptismal waters and off the mountain of bright light keep echoing across the ages. That echo is a gift. Knowing what we are made of, we often can't hear the first time what we need to hear, and hence the word needs to pass by us over and over again. This word from baptism to mountaintop reverberates long enough to teach this lesson: every moment of glorious inspiration is followed by gut-wrenching perspiration. When the echo dies down, we must read ahead. After baptismal waters we read that "right away, Jesus was led into the desert to be tempted by the devil." Right after the glorious moment when Jesus stood on the pinnacle of brightness, he announced to the disciples that he must suffer and die at the hands of religious people, and Peter took him aside and "rebuked him." And in like fashion, Jesus rebuked Peter and said that it would be so. This text needs to echo long enough for us to see that the moment of greatest spiritual excitement is followed by the greatest of temptations and agony.

Jesus was blessed in his temptation only because all the temptations he received were sneak previews of temptations he would receive in his public ministry. He was tempted to be popular by doing magic. He was tempted to be popular by having an inside track with those in power. He was tempted to put himself in the place of God. It was a good thing these things happened to him, because those were the same offers he got in public ministry.

Echoes bless us. I remember a man who went on a journey to New Mexico to stand before some stone-faced canyons and meditate and "find himself." He was looking for instant spirituality, instant gratification with life, and instant quick fixes to problems he had caused. In frustration he went before a canyon wall and yelled, "More of You. I need more of You!" And the echo came back, "More of you." In time he discovered that he was not to find life by hoarding his; he would not find life by getting more of what he has enough of; he would not find life by accumulation; he discovered that he would not find life by following the narcissistic path given by parents and approved by culture. He decided to answer the sound of his own voice coming off a wall: "More of you." I know that person well enough to tell you that he found life by giving his life to that which counts, beginning with his wife and children and extending to children at risk in ghettos. There is a blessing in echoes if we will learn to listen to our own demanding voice as it comes back to indict and then bless us.

I think of another echo. I think of a time when some sniffling disciples were buttoned down in a closed house, still afraid that there might be repercussions to the fact that they were among those who hung out with Jesus, who was now dead and two days in a tomb. I see them gathered in fear and trembling, hoping against hope of not being discovered. I picture some of the disciples going back to doing what they were doing when he found them, namely fishing. Then I think of those women who had the courage to venture out on the third day with things they used to pay homage to a dead person. And then I picture a moment when these women were astonished by angels and emptiness. They shout, "He is risen," and their voices echo off the back wall of an empty tomb.

And to this day it does not matter what you think happened or did not happen on that morning. It does not matter what the Jesus Seminar or seminary or Kazantzakis have taught you: the echo off the back wall of that empty tomb cannot be silenced and has changed the world with hope in ways we cannot comprehend. There is blessing in an echo that keeps reverberating through all our minds' best efforts and our scholars' best demystification and keeps echoing the truth that God will have the last word on life, and that last word will not be death but life beyond our wildest expectations.

Echoes can bless us, and echoes can also burden us. I am burdened today by an echo I have heard. I was seminary trained in the 1960s. I entered seminary in 1966 with my black friends calling themselves "the new Negro." Within a year they were calling themselves "Black," and then there was social consciousness around racism, militarism, and sexism. Everything "nailed down came up loose." Looking back, I realize how much I read everything but did not hear much of anything. Recently I was strangely led to begin reading again the things I could not hear at the time. I read Dr. Martin Luther King, Jr.'s "Letter from a Birmingham Jail." This letter, written on toilet paper by a man who did not have reference books, was a profound answer to a group of persons who had written him telling him that he should remain quiet and let the courts, not his voice and demonstrations of nonviolence, take care of changes in America. Dr. King told them why he could not wait and why we must not wait.

I read that letter long ago, but did not hear it until I was in the midst of people of many colors torn by the reality of racism's looming menace in the 1990s. I heard the voice of Dr. King echo off the wall of a Birmingham jail. That voice led me through a painful Lent and hope for binding with others who will put the stubborn ounces of their weight behind an inclusive gospel of love of the entire human family. I am burdened by the echo of Dr. King across decades where we cannot cite much progress at the painful points he drew attention to with his life.

I remember a man talking about the burden of an echo in his mind. He was ten years of age and was interested in cocoons and butterflies. He was given a cocoon and told to watch it unfold over the long haul. One day he watched the emerging butterfly struggle to emerge, and the struggle was too difficult. And so, to be helpful, he breathed on the emerging butterfly and finally pulled away the cocoon to let it go free, and the new creature died immediately. He tells the story to this day and declares that the hardest thing to forgive himself for is the echoing memory of that butterfly and that death made by haste.

I remember another man coming to my office and telling me of a childhood where he did not receive the same attention as those around him. He talked of late summer evenings when one by one the children were called home, and then began to sob uncontrollably as he said, "No one ever called me home." His sense of abandonment still lingers. The echoes of abandonment are the chief pain that haunts the human family at every age.

Echoes of scripture can be a blessing and a burden. We are burdened by those parts that make us confront ourselves as we are with the view of who we ought to be. And then there are those moments when we are blessed by echoes of scripture which remind us of what we must never forget.

When Jesus came out of baptismal waters and stood on the mountain of bright lights, he heard the words, "This is my beloved child, listen to him." The greatest miracle of all is the moment in baptismal waters or on the morning commute when we can suddenly hear the echo of God's voice and realize that those same words are the words God uses not only for Jesus but for us also.

May the blessing of that echo lift you to receive the love that God has always desired to give you while your attention was elsewhere. Amen.

The Best For Last

Epiphany 2 **John 2:1-11**

Come with me to a party. The party is a wedding celebration. Hard as it is for you to believe, these celebrations lasted four days with some heavy drinking involved.

At the party I want you to overhear a conversation that is going on. The conversation is between Jesus and his mother.

Mary points to the fact that there is no wine. In many marriages I know, the husband is supposed to know what to do if the wife calls attention to something. "Honey, my car is on empty." Translated, that means, "It is time for you to drive the car down to the corner and fill it up." It is indirect but effective communication.

When Mary said, "There is no wine," Jesus was to translate that into: "Do something."

Now Jesus does something that truly irritates some people. He answers a question she did not ask. Jesus answers by saying, "What concern is that of yours? My hour has not come." It must have been difficult to communicate with a son whose mind was not present at the party, but was thinking constantly about the inclusive banquet of God.

I imagine Mary giving Jesus the look that tells him that it might be far easier for him to just do what she wants than to have a conversation that goes nowhere. Then she instructs people to do exactly what Jesus says. The pots are filled with water. Wine comes forth from them. The wine steward reveals the custom of the day: "Normally at a party like this they serve the good wine first and the bad wine when everyone is drunk. You have saved the best for last!"

We are told that this was Jesus' first sign or miracle. We are told that it revealed his glory. We are told that his disciples believed.

What is it that God intended for us to give first that we give last and often reluctantly? I believe that God intends for the Church to give first to the world a celebration of diversity but, in fact, the Church falls in line with the world and celebrates likeness. And even among those congregations that profess to affirm the diversity of creation, more often than not they are saying something in the sanctuary that is quite different from their actions in the parking lot.

Let me share with you the people and the poets who have taught me the richness of diversity.

I. The People

The first to teach me about the richness of diversity were the people in a small remote Mexican village where I went with youth and building gear to construct a school. The hospitality of those people with absolutely nothing started me on a pilgrimage I have not yet completed. What is there about the generosity of the poor that so far outshines that which I find among people who have everything?

These people wanted to give us, their guests, a special treat at the end of the week. They invited us to ride their horses. I came to the corral to take my ride and saw a little sign in Spanish that I could not read. The people gathered around to see me get on this one horse that looked a little frisky. As if the gate were opened at a race, that horse took off with my lanky body bouncing everywhere and finally to the ground within 25 yards.

When I got back to the corral, I asked one of the people who spoke English to translate the sign written in Spanish. She said in halting English that it read like this:

For those who like to ride fast, we have fast horses.
For those who like to ride slow, we have slow horses.
For those who are big, we have big horses.
For those who are little, we have little horses.
For those who have never ridden horses before, we have horses THAT HAVE NEVER BEEN RIDDEN BEFORE!

The week ended with a great feast prepared by the people that would have lasted four days if we would have allowed it. They, having nothing, gave everything to us who had everything. I shall never forget their faces.

Wine was brought to us. Not great vats, but one single bottle. One man knew that on that night our Protestant group would gather for a Maundy Thursday service and that we had no grape juice or wine. He brought us the one single bottle he had left from six bottles given him ten years ago. With pride he gave it to us. Our group gathered later and had our service. I thought for a moment of the party earlier that day and I regretted not being able to be at the same communion table with these wonderful people. I knew we were separated by language and religious custom, but I still missed the fact that we were not together, as we had been at the party.

The next morning, I went early to the top of the hill where a Catholic church had been built 600 years earlier. I walked there to see the sunrise and take a picture. I thought I was alone at the entrance to the church, when suddenly I realized that there was a lady from the village standing near. She came up to me and smiled and nodded. After I took several pictures, she came to me to speak from her heart. In broken English she said, "There are many religions. But uno dios! Only one God!" That being my last year in seminary, I realized that she was giving me the most important theological lesson of all: the best we save for last is the first thing that Christ calls out in us, namely, that we celebrate the diversity of creation and the God that loves the entire creation lavishly and equally.

II. The Poets

The poets are probably our best help and chance of getting a glimpse of the life Jesus intended for us to give first, but that we too often save for last, or never get around to giving at all.

When I was a senior in high school, we produced Thornton Wilder's *Our Town*. At seventeen years of age, I thought that a play that had a stage manager talking to the crowd along with people from the graveyard was pure craziness. The problem was that at seventeen I had not experienced heartburn, let alone the loss of someone I love. So my problem was that I could not hear the play rightly. Now that I have seen friends my own age die, I can hear the words of Emily as she comes back from the grave to relive one day.

Emily asks the stage manager, "Do any human beings ever realize life while they live it? Every, every minute?" The stage manager says, "No. The saints and poets, maybe — they do some." A man from the grave says, "Yes, now you know. Now you know! That's what it was to be alive. To move about in a cloud of ignorance; to go up and down trampling on the feelings of those ... of those about you. To spend and waste time as though you had a million years. To be always at the mercy of one self-centered passion or another. Now you know ... that's the happy existence you wanted to go back to, ignorance and blindness." Then another man speaks from the grave and says, "That ain't the whole truth and you know it."

Another poet reminds us of the richness of diversity. W. H. Auden in his "Christmas Oratorio" points to the One who draws all together. Auden says, "He is the Way. Follow Him through the Land of Unlikeness; you will see rare beasts, and have unique adventures. He is the Truth. Seek Him in the Kingdom of Anxiety; You will come to a great city that has expected your return for years. He is the Life. Love Him in the World of the Flesh; And at your marriage all its occasions shall dance for joy."

The Talmud says, "In the world to come, each of us will be called to account for all the good things God put on earth which we refuse to enjoy." What is that human spirit that leads us to bow down and worship at the feet of likeness, when the glory of God's presence is found in the differences?

I remember reading Graham Greene's book, *The Potting Shed*, where he tells of Anna, who is afraid to wander through the garden nearby. "I've had such a funny dream. I was going down the path to the potting shed, and there was an enormous lion there fast asleep." Her friend James asks, "What did you do?" "I woke him up," said Anna. "Did he eat you?" asked James cautiously. "No," said Anna. "He licked my hand."

We get off track in life and think that a nightmare is living with differences, so we worship at the altar of sameness. In fact our fears are transformed to faith by facing that which scares us most and finding there the blessing God has desired to give us from the beginning of time.

We save for last what God wants us to give first, and that is our open hearts and minds given to the work of embracing diversity. The first miracle symbolically calls our attention to that fact. God wants us to begin by embracing diversity, and it is the last thing we get around to, if at all.

And still Christ gladly comes after we have tried everything and have been left wanting. Christ comes and invites us to the true miracle that he wishes for the human family. Christ comes when the pupil is exhausted and finally ready and reveals the truth only the poet can give.

> *After the seas are all cross'd, (as they seem already cross'd)*
> *After the great captains and engineers have accomplish'd their work,*
> *After the noble inventors, after the scientists, the chemist, the geologist, ethnologist,*
> *Finally shall come the poet worthy of that name,*
> *The true son of God shall come singing his songs.*
>
> Walt Whitman

May we sing the song that praises the God who comes in the unfamiliar and blesses us with new wine and new life. Amen.

Deep Joy For
A Shallow World

Epiphany 3 *Luke 4:14-21*
(and Nehemiah 8:1-4a, 5-6, 8-10)

I bring you good news of deep joy in a shallow world. No matter how many fears and failures you bring to this place; no matter how many times you have to pick yourself up or be picked up after knowing deep pain; no matter how difficult it has been to get through an average day, let alone life itself; no matter what — God is leading us to deep joy that is eternal in a world that is focused on entertainment.

Our main attention is given to Nehemiah, who was called to lead a people out of total disaster physically while Ezra was leading the people out of disaster spiritually. We have here the political and the practical. We have the prophetic and the prayerful. To people caught between ultimate allegiance to God and burdens of the present order, Nehemiah says, "Go your way; eat; give to those who don't have anything to eat; do not grieve; the joy of the Lord is your strength!"

In a world where we seek instant gratification it is hard to hear this word that talks about ultimate rather than immediate things. People are deeply desirous of joy that goes beyond the current treadmill of daily life. The biblical word indicates that such joy is not to be found *in* what happens to us, but in *seeing through* what happens to us toward an ultimate victory in the midst of temporary defeats. Gratitude is not *for* what happens to us but *in spite of* what happens to us. That is why Paul speaks of "peace that passes understanding." If you are going to wait to think your way into acting differently, you never will. Instead, Paul asks us to *act our way into a new way of thinking.*

I see a boy at his Bar Mitzvah, many years after Ezra and Nehemiah. The boy watches the Hasidic masters come forward as he reads and watches them place a drop of honey on the page he reads. He asks what that is for. They reply, "It stands for the sweetness of knowing God's joy and the joy God intends for us in the midst of the struggles and pain of life."

Deep joy comes in a shallow world in several ways.

I. Joy comes on the other side of our demand for justice.

Psalm 30 says, "Weeping may linger for the night, but joy comes with the morning." The long night for many people is the night they are demanding justice in the world, when all along what the world needs, and what God gives, is mercy.

There was a woman who hired an expensive artist to do her portrait. The artist had her sit several times with him and then he went off and finished the work. He came with the portrait and presented it. The woman looked at it and said, "This portrait does not do my face justice." The artist replied, "Your face doesn't need justice; it needs mercy."

And so do we. Justice is getting what you deserve. Mercy is getting what you need even though you don't know in the moment that you need it. Jack Benny received an award one time. In his sketches on television he was famous for being really tight with his money. In private life he was incredibly generous with many causes. When he received the award he said, "I don't deserve this award. On the other hand, I have arthritis, and I don't deserve that either."

We begin life wanting justice. Joy comes when we grant the same mercy to others that we insist on having for ourselves. Most often we are not merciful because we have not allowed God's mercy to touch us. You can't give what you do not have. "Love your neighbor AS YOU LOVE YOURSELF" has a warning that you can't give what you do not have. Too often we don't hear or heed that warning.

When visiting the big island of Hawaii, I was deeply moved by the City of Refuge. Here was a place where persons could come if they were being sought by an enemy, including the government, and not be harmed there. When they reached that place they were forgiven, restored to community, and turned back into the world. I think they did there what we hoped the confessional booth would do throughout history. I believe that for the most part we refuse forgiveness to others because we have not first ourselves visited the City of Refuge, where we are loved just as we are and not as we ought to be. The deep joy promised biblically is ours in the moment that we make a visit to the City of Refuge and then give the same mercy to others.

II. Joy comes on the other side of the fences we build.

Joy is ours when we move the fences we've inherited. During World War I there were some Americans passing through an area of France. One of their friends was killed, and they wanted a place to bury him. They found a local church with a cemetery around it and inquired if the man could be buried there. The priest asked if the man was Catholic. They said he was not. The priest apologized for the fact that it was a Catholic cemetery, but was also compassionate. "Why don't you fellows bury him just outside the fence." They agreed and did so.

Several weeks later the men were traveling through the area and wanted to visit the grave. They came to the graveyard and for some reason could not find the grave. They went to the door of the rectory and asked the priest. "We can't find the grave. What happened?" The priest looked rather sheepish when he said, "After you came that day and buried him outside the fence, I found that I could not sleep. And so I got out of bed and moved the fence to include the grave of your friend."

I have had people tell me that story could not happen. I am here to tell you that it did. The joy of God comes when, after reading all the rules, we rewrite them in our daily lives to be inclusive of all.

What happened in the cross of Jesus Christ? God moved the fence to include all people but the church that represents that cross has spent an inordinate amount of time seeking to put a fence in front of what Jesus gave to all of us. "For freedom Christ has set you free." To anyone who can hear those words, whether Protestant or Catholic, whether Buddhist or Islamic, they will know in an instant that the Holy is present anytime anyone moves fences to include all people.

III. Joy comes on the other side of surrender.

Weekly I stand before people with pain I cannot heal or fix and whose pain moves me to numbed silence. As a matter of fact, I am convinced that no person should be allowed to preach each week unless he or she has sat with persons who experience pain that will not be cured by simple formulae or slick "ten things you need to do" lists.

I know a woman who surrendered. She surrendered to the fact that blindness would invade her life and there was nothing anyone could do about it. As her blindness came slowly upon her, she came to me one time and demanded (she did not ask) that I pray for her healing. She did not want some fancy "inner healing" talk, and she didn't want to talk about the many faces of healing that clergy are prone to talk about. She wanted the "lay your hands on me and let me walk away with new sight" kind of healing.

I understood what she was asking for. Then came two surrendering moments. I surrendered to doing exactly what she wanted. One moment in a private chapel we prayed, and I made it very clear to God that we wanted her to go out with new vision.

We left the chapel. I inquired of her several times in the days ahead, wondering if anything was different. She seemed very unconcerned to talk about her sight. It was as if it did not matter. Finally, three months later I asked her if she was seeing any differently. She squinted and said she could not tell. Then she said, "What I asked for is not what I got, but was what I needed. I needed release from my fear. I needed release from the worry that my husband would not find me attractive and that my children would be doomed to show me through the dark. After that moment, I could see no better with my eyes, but now can see perfectly with my soul. I wanted sight. In relief from my fear, I got that."

What we ask for in life is not always what we get, but it is what we would have asked for in the first place had we known.

Joy comes on the other side of surrender.

Those who are in most need for moving toward surrender are those who have lost loved ones and whose memories are not healed by their own accord. Those who have lost loved ones and have grieved for what seems a lifetime are also people who have found healing not by their own effort, but by their daring to keep showing up for life. The gift that death is not a wall but a door, that death is not a fence but a gate, comes to grieving persons by ways we cannot know. To go the way that we cannot know is called the spiritual discipline of surrender.

IV. Joy comes on the other side of seeking a treasure.

I love the Hasidic tale about Isak of Krakow. Isak, the young Jewish man, wanted to build a temple to God. He was poor and without money. One night he had a dream. In the dream he was instructed to go to Prague, the great capital, and dig under the bridge that went into the king's house and there he would find gold.

So he went. He arrived in Prague and was digging under the bridge when he was found by a guard. He decided in a split second that he should tell the truth. He told the guard that he had a dream of the gold and had come to dig. The guard began to laugh. "Why just last night I had a dream. I dreamt that in Krakow there was a man by the name of Isak, and if I were to go to his home and move his stove and dig under the floor, I would find gold. Now do you think I am so stupid as to go there to that Jewish city with hundreds of men named Isak and look for gold?" Isak was released and began the long journey home. Upon arriving he went into the house, moved the stove, dug in the dirt under the stove and discovered gold with which he built a temple to God. The moral of the story is that what you want and need is near you, but most often you must go on a long journey in order to find it.

Joy comes when we stop seeking treasure and see the treasure of everyday life, and live with the knowledge that in the sight of God we are the treasure. A woman wrote once about a precious vase that her mother owned. It was "the family treasure." Then one day the child accidentally bumped it and knocked it to the floor and into a million pieces. She screamed in terror of being punished. The mother ran into the room and said, "What's wrong?" "I broke it," said the horrified child. "I broke the family treasure." The mother was immediately relieved and, picking up the pieces, said, "It does not matter. I thought you were hurt." The woman telling the story said, "It was at that moment that I knew that I was the family treasure, and it made all the difference in my life."

Joy comes on the other side of seeking treasure and in realizing that the one who made you delights in you forever. That knowledge does not lessen what happens to us in life, but it lifts us with the knowledge that "weeping may linger for the night, but joy will come in the morning."

Most of life is built backwards. We think that we must seek joy rather than let joy find us. We think we need and must have more of what we have enough of. In fact the greatest joy is to be found in the everyday moments when we allow God to find us. Spiritual arrogance is the attitude that we can find God. Time tells us that when we are willing to go to the places of service and caring, God finds us there with deep and indescribable joy.

The good news is that it is not up to us to find God. Instead, God is in search of us and God always will have his way. We will be found.

Many of us were troubled by the new milk cartons that came out, each of them having the picture of a child who was missing. A child was asking his parents about the lost children. Then he asked a more important question: "What would you do if I was missing?" The mother bent over the child, looked him in the face, and said, "If you were ever missing, don't forget that we would never, ever, ever stop looking for you."

The words of that parent are the words of God. God sees us when lost and will stoop as low as our lostness, as low as a manger, to tell us that God will never stop searching until we are found.

May God grant us the deep joy of being found by the One who comes to give us life in abundance. Amen.

Edges

Epiphany 4   ***Luke 4:21-30***

"**Life** is a daring adventure or it is nothing." Helen Keller said that, a lady robbed of her sight, hearing, and ability to speak. She was saying that life is to be lived on the edge, or not at all.

There is a difference between living on the edge and being what we call an "edgy" or irritable person. Jesus was on the edge at all times, and only once can I recall when he was edgy. That moment was when he went storming into the Temple, white-hot with rage, and made a whip and turned over tables. Matthew, Mark, and Luke have this happening in his last week alive. John has him turning the tables at the beginning of his ministry, just after his first miracle. I don't care when it happened, I just know it happened that Jesus was edgy in the Temple. Why? Because the mysterious God of Moses, who came in wonder on the mountaintop of old, was suddenly reduced to formulae and a few shekels. Jesus was mad and edgy over the way we worship, more than over the daily violations of the love commandment and the Ten Commandments.

But that is not our text nor what we will talk about here. We will not talk about Jesus being occasionally edgy, but the fact that he lived on the edge. Jesus lived on the margins and moved the margins to include all people, and hence invited hostile crowds to want to edge him out of existence. Today the church wants to edge Jesus out of our worship anytime the margins are made too wide and include too many who are not like us. Recently I was sitting at my computer, contemplating the way Jesus offended so many people so quickly in his ministry. I asked, "Why?" The answer was at the top of my screen. My word processing instructions at the top read: "Drag the margin boundaries on the rulers." That is why he upset people so much: in his life he dragged the margin boundaries of race, creed, and color to include all people. He dragged the margin boundaries when he gave a common meal, which we have made a holy meal symbolic of his inclusive love for all people. Jesus is dragged to the edge of a cliff to be put out of the lives of his townspeople because no one wants the margins of daily living to be inclusive of strangers.

In a way, Jesus was led to the edge of the cliff for doing the same thing that gives us the greatest honor when we are young. Jesus was run out of town for reading and interpreting scripture. I can still remember the day my mentor in ministry tapped me on the shoulder and asked me to read the morning scripture. It was because I was the only kid in the youth group wearing a tie that day. I got in the pulpit and felt a small tug that invited me to stay there. When anyone asks me how I got into the ministry, I must go back to the time in my home church when I was asked to read scripture and stand in the pulpit. I discovered I couldn't leave it.

Jesus did not get into trouble for *reading* the word but for *interpreting* the word. It is one thing to read the "word." It is another to **be** "the word" that brings God's grace, judgment, and ethical obedience into focus. The one whose words and deeds are the same makes people edgy and makes people want to push them over the edge and run them out of their temples that have long been tamed and tranquilized into manageable form.

We are invited to live on the edge of language. God exists beyond our best language and we witness to God best by living rather than by language. I think of the greatest attempts of all the theologians and can read most of what was written without a single chill or desire to follow after the One to whom they point.

On the other hand, I look at the living of others and cannot forget the life they invite me to in their living out the word. In

India Gandhi stepped on the train one day, and one of his shoes slipped off and landed on the track. He was unable to retrieve it as the train took off. To the amazement of his companions, Gandhi calmly took off his other shoe and threw it back along the track near the other shoe. Asked by the folks aboard the train why he did it, Gandhi smiled and said, "The poor man who finds the shoe lying on the track will now have a pair he can use." This is living on the edge that challenges so deeply the way we have been known to live that we want to edge the source of that way out of our lives forever.

I remember the story of Theophane the Monk. He was traveling along a path one day and ran into a young man. He asked the young man where he was going. The young man replied, "I am looking for the pearl of great price." Theophane said calmly, "Well, look no more. I have it." Theophane produced the pearl of great price. The young man was in pure delight to see and find what he was looking for. Then Theophane said, "Here, take it." And he gave the young man the pearl of great price. The young man was delighted and danced for awhile and then sat under a tree to contemplate. "The pearl of great price! I have it! But is it better to have it or to have the ability to give it away like Theophane the Monk? How long will this question rob me of my joy?"

God calls us to live on the edge, not with ancient word recited and unlived, but with a living word to be given away in us and recited in the rituals of daily life.

We have just waded through the season of Advent, a season of waiting. Now we are on the final steps in Epiphany, and I think there comes a time that we ask, "What are you waiting for?" You are invited to the edge to let your light shine. If you knew you were going to die in thirty days, what would you do in those thirty days, and *why are you not doing that right now*? The butterfly lives only thirty days, yet there is enough time for the things that are truly important.

May God help us to make friends with the light entrusted to us and walk to the edge of daily living and give it in Christ's name. Amen.

Is It Better To Catch Or Be Caught?

Epiphany 5　　　　　　　　　　　　　　　　　　*Luke 5:1-11*

As a boy I was never good at catching things, except a cold now and then. I tried to catch a pony to ride and failed. The butterfly trip was a disaster. I tried catching frogs but didn't try too hard because I didn't know what I would do with them once I caught them. Fish weren't my favorite for eating, so catching them was no treat, because I knew it implied that I would eat them with delight rather than gagging on them, which I always did. I never was good at catching things.

A major church denomination has as its theme, "Catch the Spirit." As usual, the church got it backward. We are not to set our sights at catching or getting, but allowing ourselves to be caught. We are invited to be caught by a spirit that helps us make a giving instead of a living.

The greatest spiritual arrogance is seen in the language of "catching." People are in search of God and will write endless numbers of books telling one how to find God. The truth of the gospel is that we cannot find God, but there are places we can go and things we can do *where God can find us*! The joy in Christian living is not in the catching but in the vulnerability of being caught by the one who made us in the first place. Catch the spirit? No! You can't. Be caught by the spirit? Of course! Life begins there.

How can we be caught by the spirit and set free through service and surrender rather than self-absorption and control?

First, we can be caught by the spirit when we change our language. I think of the Prodigal Son as a story that tells about the most important of spiritual journeys. His journey begins when he demands, "Give me now what is supposed to come to me later." His journey ends and life begins when he says, "Make me as one of your servants." And we know that story is ours also. We live in a world that teaches us very well to get more of what we have enough of without asking if all that stuff is getting us where we want and need to be. We don't often know how to question whether this way truly leads to the life we want. Many painful moments have to come about before we realize that life is to be found in the giving, not in the living for oneself alone. Our journey is like the prodigal's, from "give me" to "make me a servant of the things that really matter."

Second, we can be caught by the spirit when we realize the gift of each other. Do you remember the words given by George Burns in the movie *Oh, God*? When asked why God starves children, Burns responds by saying, "I don't. You do. I gave you enough food to go around, but you won't share it. I gave you all you need. Then I gave you the gift of each other." What has to happen for us to see each other as a gift?

Susan Lawley was a vice president at Goldman Sachs, with a salary in six figures, a fine husband, a delightful eleven-year-old son, two houses, and vacations each year in Europe. She was driving home late one night, which was the usual routine. She was driving in the dark. We don't know why, but sometimes we can see more clearly when it is dark. Susan began to cry uncontrollably, and finally she stopped along the road. She would reflect later, "I realized that tonight, like almost every night, I would miss seeing my son because he was already in bed. I realized that life is too short to live like that." She quit her job immediately and became a consultant working out of her home and things worked out quite well.

It is so hard for us to be caught by the spirit when we are caught by a job that takes us away from all things important. Scott Turow in his book *Pleading Guilty* has a passage that most who are caught in the trap of travel do not want to hear. "Now it's a badge of status to be away from home four nights a week. But on God's green planet, is there anything more depressing than an empty hotel room at ten at night, and the thought that work, privilege, economic need not only claim the daylight hours but have, however briefly, entitled you to these awesome lonesome instants in which you're remote from the people and the things, tiny, loved and familiar, that sustain a life?"

Henry David Thoreau gave us words we still have not heard yet when he said, "Money is not required to buy one thing necessary (for) the soul." That is a saying close to the one that reminds us that "in heaven there is no one there who says, 'I wish I would have spent more time at the office.'"

Sometimes people are caught by this spirit over the long haul and others are caught all at once. There was a man who was awakened out of a deep sleep and realized he was ignoring the faces near him, his wife's and his children's. He decided to change immediately. He left work early, got some flowers and champagne, and came home unannounced to his astonished wife, who answered the door. She looked at him and began crying uncontrollably. "What's wrong?" he inquired after seeing that she did not respond with the enthusiasm he had hoped for. She said, "The kids have been crying, my mother has been griping over the phone, the shower is broken, I need groceries and can't get out, and then you come home drunk!"

There might be some adjustment, but finally there is great joy when we realize the gift of each other. Grace comes in the form of enough time to let others in your life know that they are a gift to you.

Third, we get caught by the spirit when we realize that the human family lives more by affirmation than it does by bread.

I read about an African tribe who had a very interesting way of disciplining people who had done something wrong in the village. When a person was found to have done a misdeed, the entire village would come out and surround that person. One by one the villagers would shout out, not what the person did wrong, but what good things the person had done in the past. Once they bombarded that person with the goodness they had seen in him, they released the person to begin all over again, mindful that the bad deed was an aberration and not a permanent state of being. Name the last time you saw a human being become good by telling him how bad he is. May our sophisticated society be smart enough to learn the lesson from this primitive village!

The power of the gospel is that the love we can experience in family or village is the same kind God envisions us giving to the stranger. Simone Weil said, "Love is acting toward the people we do not know, and hence cannot love, as though they were the people we actually do love." We don't think our way into acting this way, but act our way into this new way of thinking that was seen in the one who asked his disciples to "go deeper" into the water and into life. Live more deeply by moving the margins of village and family to include love for the stranger, who is not a stranger in the eyes of our all-inclusive God.

Jesus invites us to dwell deeply. He invites us not to catch the spirit as Jesus commanded them to catch fish. Instead, Jesus invites us to allow ourselves to be caught by *the* spirit. That spirit allows us to dwell deeply when we change our language from "give me" to "make me"; when we realize the gift of each other; when we realize that the human family lives more by affirmation than they do by bread.

I close with this. Seldom will a minister ever quote from Gypsy Rose Lee, the famous burlesque queen, and perhaps this will be my only time. She declared once, "God is love. But get it in writing." Those of us who once sought to "catch the spirit" and now are "caught by the spirit" are those who can say something differently. In looking back, we can say, "God is love and we got it in writing. It is written in ink. Red ink. And it is not ink."

May God help us to be caught by the one whose narrow way leads to full life on roads less traveled. Amen.

Flatliners

Epiphany 6   *Luke 6:17-26*

What would happen if on this Sunday we were to come to Jesus and ask, "Tell us flat-out what you're about?" Jesus might, on this particular day, say, "I have come to give comfort to the uncomfortable and to make uncomfortable those who have comfort." He has a way of flattening things out. Jesus is a flatliner.

What if we were to ask that question of the entire Bible? "Don't give me the six-week course. Just give me a compendium of that battered and complex book. What does it look like?" He would have to say, "God made the world in love, and for some unknown reason, the human family rejects that love and chooses to go in a different direction. God will not reject the world that rejects God. God continues a mysterious and relentless pursuit of us to the end of time." This is the "flat-out" bottom line of the Gospel.

In the Gospel of Luke, it says that Jesus went down to the flats and began to speak to the people. The Gospel of Matthew would find Jesus going to the hill. But on both the mount and the flats the message is the same. He gives us the flatline. He levels with them. He flattens every category of the human family. And if you can't hear that in the text, you can't hear it rightly. Finally, all of us are on a level place; all are on one level with the Gospel. Jesus flattens out all categories. We all receive the same blessings and demands. It's not doled out according to our abilities, our good looks, or our charm. Everything's flattened out by the message that Jesus gives on the plains.

It's a difficult world that we live in right now. It's kind of a confusing world when all of the traditional roles have been flattened out. We don't know which end is up most of the time. What can we say of traditional roles? I was told, "Just be a good boy, go off to college, and you'll have a career that you'll stay with the rest of your life." That turned out not to be the case for most of the persons in my generation. They have had at least three careers. Somebody said, "This generation will have twelve." I felt that we owed it to our children to send them to college, but they don't know exactly what to do with their education. It's a totally different world. The roles make it even more complex. What are the roles of men and women? What's the mix?

I love the story about a boy and a girl who were trying to find a game that they could play together. The boy was picking out games he thought he was good at. He said, "I'd like to play some baseball." She said, "NO, you're a little better and I haven't been on a girls' baseball team. I don't want to do that."

"How about football?"

"No. Way too rough. You guys tackle. I don't want to do that."

"Well, how about soccer?"

"Well, I've played that, but I don't think that's the one."

So, the boy, who's trying to be accommodating and find out what these new roles are, finally turns to her and says, "Why don't we play house?"

She said, "That's great! I'll be the daddy."

In our text, the blessings begin. People are healed of diseases; the troubled are cured; the unclean spirits are cast out. People touched Jesus as He went by. I like the text. It says, "All of them knew that He loved them." Magic! So far, it's good. There are more blessings. The poor will get the kingdom! The hungry are going to be filled. If you weep — you'll laugh. Those hated and excluded on account of me will have joy and reward in heaven!

Then comes the bad news.

Jesus says, "Woe to you rich." Everyone of us is among the five percent wealthy in the world. So none of us can escape. "Woe to you, Dick, and the rest of you. You've already got all you're going to get." The question is: "Is just getting things all you really want?"

"Woe to you who are full. You're going to be hungry later." The point is: our hunger is only fixed when we have paid attention to the hunger of the spirit and fed that.

"Woe to you who are laughing. You're going to cry." Only those who think of others as much as themselves really know how to laugh. When life is over, God will have the last word. It will all be restored. All of the lame will be restored. All of those things that you have loved and lost will be restored. This is good news. That's why we laugh. But on a daily basis oftentimes we don't have a reason to laugh. When we laugh it is because we know the last word will be restoration.

"Woe to you with a good reputation." Big deal. The false prophets had a good reputation. Is that really what you want? Be very careful, because even after these edicts are given by Jesus, He's still in a flatliner mode. He flattens us all out. He takes us all on the level. He puts every category on an even keel. Please hear this or you will miss the gospel message here. I have known in my life some very wealthy people in whom I have seen the highest spiritual heights and I have also seen those heights in some very poor people. In my life I have found the worst in both rich and poor. We're still flatlining. Being rich and being poor is not the object of the gospel message today, and if you think it is, you'll miss the real message.

Instead, there's something else. What is it? It's the lens. After making us all equal, Jesus wants us to see everything with new and different eyes.

Hasid was called in to his rabbi. He said, "You rang? You want me?"

"Yes, we need to talk."

You see, Hasid was rich and didn't share his wealth, and everybody in the temple knew it. So the rabbi brought him into his home and took him to a window and said, "Tell me what you see."

He said, "I see a piece of glass and through it I can see all of the people walking up and down the road."

"Very good. Now come over here. What do you see here?"

"This is a mirror and in it I can only see myself."

And then the rabbi looked at him and said, "Do you know what the difference is between these two pieces of glass? One of them has been coated with silver."

And it seems that within the human family, once we have coated ourselves with silver, we can only see ourselves. It doesn't have to be. Jesus flattened us out so that all of us are capable of being able to see as He wants us to see, every human being equal in the sight of God. So the rabbi told Hasid to get a new lens.

Through the lens of Jesus, I can hear the voice of Christ speaking to us even in this moment: "If you had only six months to live, what would you do, and if you're not doing it right now, why not?" It's the lesson for all of us. There are people in our midst, even right now, who are teaching us that lesson, if we will receive it; who live daily in the flux and flow, wondering if the next day will come. Listen to them because in them is the voice of the kingdom. If all of us are not living that way, then why not?

So Jesus helps us to see through some things. Jesus helps us **to see through our persistent pain, because it is the common uniting factor of all of us.**

We're united here. We are united by our pain. Sometime in our lives, all of our losses are going to be exactly the same. Ah, we know that in the back of our minds. We are all one people in our pain. It's the common link.

The church which I served in San Diego was right on the edge of a large gay/lesbian community. Our door was open to them. We never found a lot of persons coming to our church, because there was another church that was largely made up of gay and lesbian persons. As we'd interview them and invite them to church, they'd say, "We're more comfortable elsewhere." I remember a man who had bumped into me on the street and later called me at the church. I didn't remember exactly who he was. "Would you come to my home?" he asked. I said, "Sure." I went there and discovered that he was bedridden. He was not well. Sitting on a chest of drawers was one of those frames that has six holes in it for six different pictures. Five of the holes were empty. I said, "Do you want to tell me about that?" He said, "I have lost five of my friends this year. I can no longer bear to look at their faces in front of me, and I had to take them down, and hold their memories in my life. And now, I, too, am dying." I went back to the church. I assigned a Stephen Minister, who had lost a sister and three other of her closest friends during the last year. They knew that they had a common language in their losses which Jesus has promised He will march us through.

I read recently about a nineteenth century soldier who saw with the lens of Jesus. On a memorial that was dedicated to him at St. Paul's Cathedral in London, it says, "To Charles George Gordon, who always and everywhere gave his strength to the weak, his substance to the poor, his sympathy to the suffering, and his heart to God." What a marvelous tribute! What a marvelous description of the lens through which we are invited to see the world. Jesus' pain in the midst of all of us is the pain of putting all of these things in front of the people and the people still insisting on blindness.

I have a friend who talks about the disciples being the "chosen frozen." They were the persons who really didn't see what was there. He wrote a column that said, "I can just see Jesus speaking to them on the plains, speaking to them on the levee, and Peter speaks first, 'Are we supposed to write this down, Jesus?' James says, 'Will we have a test?' And Philip says, 'I don't have any paper.' Bartholomew says, 'Do we have to turn this in?' John says, 'The other disciples didn't have to learn this.' Matthew says, 'May I be excused for the men's room?' Judas says, 'What does this have to do with real life?' And then there's a Pharisee that represents many of us who says, 'Where are your anticipatory set and your objectives in the cognitive domain?'" And it is at that moment that Jesus wept. He wept not because of unkindness. Jesus weeps over Jerusalem and over the chosen frozen because of the many times that we wrap ourselves up in meetings that do not matter, dealing with splitting hairs of theology and other things that do not matter. Thank God we have this place where we are not so much committed to the theological hair splitting as we are to the common suffering of the human family and giving ourselves to that common pain. Jesus helps us. He helps us see our common pain. He gives us a new lens.

There's a novel about a missionary who is being held prisoner. The man who was holding him was involved in a revolution that he wasn't too clear about. So the missionary, who seemed to take a certain kind of delight in prison, started questioning the guard. He asked the guard what he was about and shook the guard's foundation greatly. The missionary said, "What do you want? What do you really want in life? What is your revolution about?" And the man said in a vague way, "I think I want to be comfortable." You know, we teach our children this. Who will teach them the lens of Jesus to make friends with their uncomfortable side, and the things that are said to them from the mouth of Jesus that should make all of us uncomfortable? Love, according to Jesus, is the willingness to become uncomfortable for the sake of somebody else. Do we really want comfort for our children? It's in the process of giving ourselves away to things that count that we are given all of these things that the gospel promises. We're supposed to know these things. But we teach contentment.

What if Edison's parents had taught him to be contented? What if Edison's parents had taught him the shame of failure? He had 99 failures before creating the light bulbs that illumine us in this very moment. Is contentment what we really want to teach?

What do we do? We create false theology. We sit around in discussion groups and say, "I think we ought to ask the question, 'Why does God make people naked and poor?' God, why don't You do something about it?" And God answers, "I did do something about it. I gave them you." And still we don't want to hear. I am praying in my own life right now for young people in our congregation, for that matter for young people everywhere. I pray for them everyday to have "divine discontent." Young people have been coming into my office, saying, "I just don't know what to do." "I'm a sophomore." "I'm a junior." "I'm in college." "I just don't know what I want to do with my life." I say, "Great. This is a great opportunity." I would like us to be able to say to that young person in that moment, "How would you like to clear up that question or work on that question by working among the poor in India? How would you like us to send you to South America? How would you like us to have you build houses among the poor in Mexico?

You can clear up your question in that way." I don't believe that theology today should be done from the perspective of anything else, but among the perspective of those who are poor. Invite young people to serve in those kinds of places and they will come back, I think, with different problems, problems that they might be thankful for. I would pray for our young people that they will have divine discontentment and that we will help them by sending them away in service.

In the last century Henry David Thoreau asked the question I've wanted to ask and have not had the courage to ask. He gave me the courage. When the telegraph was first put into use, he said, "My understanding is that somehow it was strung from Boston to Texas. I don't know how it got that way, but they sent a message across and it went in the newspaper that instantaneously you could send a message across that wire and it would get there right away." Henry David Thoreau said, "Yes, this is amazing that we can communicate that way." And then he said, "I wonder if the person communicating had anything important to say?"

Now we have the superhighway of information. I was told in seminary that this was coming and now it's here. I like my little CD-ROM. I like all that information. I like all the access, but there's a question dangling out there: "Do we really have something that important to say?" Persons inside the Church should be the first to be able to say, "Yes we do and it's totally counter to our culture. We do have something that says, 'Happy will you be when you pay attention to this and this and this' " — all of these things that Jesus said on the plain. Henry David Thoreau was just bringing up the fact that we can create all of this stuff and totally miss the ideals of the kingdom.

Charles Laughton faced that question one time and was able to deal with it in a way that we might want. He was in Nebraska speaking to a group of people. He was quoting Shakespeare and all kinds of other literature. He made a mistake one night. He began quoting scripture and people started fidgeting around and becoming disinterested. All of a sudden, right in the middle of quoting from scripture, he quit and sat down. There was a man in the audience who pointed to an uneducated farmer in Nebraska and said,

"Mr. Laughton, would you allow him to recite scripture?" And that man in coveralls came to the platform and recited by heart Psalm 23. Laughton had the courage to say, "I came to you and I knew the words, but I've seen now a man who knows the author."

We have been entrusted with knowing that difference. If we don't know that difference we need to decipher that difference and to seek it with our whole hearts. What is the difference God wants in us? The courage to create the life of the spirit, in a culture that turns its back on it, by getting people to look through the lens of heaven. And then, for those kinds of people, it may be said, like a paraphrase I read of Psalm 1:

> *Blessed are the man and the woman,*
> *the young person, the child.*
> *Blessed are they who have grown beyond their greed*
> *and put an end to their hatred*
> *and no longer nourish illusions.*
> *But they delight in the way things are*
> *and keep their hearts open, day and night.*
> *They are like trees planted near flowing rivers,*
> *which bear fruit when they are ready.*
> *Their leaves will not fall or wither.*

Everything they do, everything these people do will succeed, finally, if not immediately!

And Jesus came down to the flats, leveled us all out, loved us the same, and saved us! May we be anxious to share this good news. Amen.

Love Your Enemies —
It Will Drive Them Crazy

Epiphany 7   *Luke 6:27-38*

It takes a steady hand to carry a full glass of water. It takes an even steadier heart to carry forgiveness to one who holds you in opposition.

In the Old Testament I like the story of Joseph, particularly its outcome. Joseph is the favored one. The older brothers say, "Dad always liked you best." In this case it was true. The brothers go out and fake Joseph's death. They bring back some bloodied clothes and say to their father, "He is dead." In actuality they have sold him into slavery in Egypt. Time passes. Famine comes to Israel. These brothers are forced to go to Egypt and ask the king for food. Traditionally, the king has been their enemy. Can you imagine the drama of that moment when they lift up their eyes and see their brother? There is an exchange and the very last line is the most important. Joseph looks upon them with the eyes of forgiveness and says, "You intended what you did to me as something that would create evil, but God and I were able to bend it into something good." You see, the noblest revenge is to forgive your enemy, and it is perhaps the last of the lessons that we learn from Jesus.

The words of Jesus that we would like to duck most are the ones in front of us, the ones about forgiving enemies. They are so difficult. Fred Craddock, a good teacher of New Testament and preaching, was teaching an undergraduate course in Oklahoma on the Gospels of Jesus. He was taking the simple writings of Jesus and putting them plainly in front of his students. There was a girl sitting in the back of the class, and as he came to the part about loving your enemies, she stood up and started slamming her books all around. She started mumbling, "Jesus and the losers. I hate Jesus and the losers. I can't stand this." She stuffed her bag and went out still mumbling, "Jesus and a bunch of losers, forgiving their enemies."

Do you remember Reginald Denny who was beaten senseless, almost to death, in Los Angeles? We remember the trial, the riots, and the controversy. But do you remember the fact that in the courtroom he was with the families of those who had beaten him? He had gathered together with them in their homes and had gotten to know them because he realized the only hope for the world was for us to forgive our aggressors. Outside the courtroom, after Denny pronounced forgiveness on those who harmed him, one newspaper man simply said, "Remember Mr. Denny had brain damage ..." So, we call someone brain-damaged who simply follows the command to love our enemies!

There was a young man who came to me after the early service one morning. He had been visiting this church for about three weeks, and he was very intrigued by this text. He said to me, "You know I like the way you talked about this text. I have entertained being a Christian for a long period of time and I still don't know if I am." I said, "Well, join the club because somewhere in what you said is my story, too." We don't so much become a Christian at one particular time in our lives as we constantly come together entertaining the notion. We are constantly in process. It is not an event that happens. Our baptism is not an end; it is a beginning that will leave us stumbling all our lives, stumbling hopefully by some mystery into doing the word that causes us so much difficulty. And still this word remains. "Humanity is never so beautiful as when praying for forgiveness or else forgiving another" (Richter).

Look at the Lord's prayer. We pray it every week and yet it is so dangerous. We become so familiar with it, it is as if we own it. But in the moment that we own it, we can't hear it, and we certainly can't do it. If only we could stand away from the Lord's prayer in such a way that it would be received new every time we say it.

My friend Glen had a man who came to him, wrestling with forgiveness. "I can't. I just can't forgive. I just can't do it." You know that emotion. We all know it. He asked Glen, "How can you help me?" Glen said, "Well, why don't you pray the Lord's prayer each day and then for the next thirty days list all of your trespasses that need forgiveness. Then I want you to come back to me in thirty days, and we'll talk about the trespasses that you feel you need to forgive in another that you don't feel you can." You know the rest of the lesson already. Oddly enough the lists will look very much the same. That is the deeper truth that resides here.

Let's look in three directions at what I call the paradox of forgiveness. Any of you who thinks you are suddenly going to go out and forgive anyone who offends you, doesn't understand this text. It is deeply paradoxical and deeply difficult, and it is not for children. It is time for us to grow up.

I. The truth hurts at the very moment that it heals us.

That's the truth in paradox. Carlisle Marney said, "The truth makes you flinch before it makes you free." "You shall know the truth and the truth shall set you free." Yes, but it makes me so mad before it sets me free. That's the paradox of the truth. It was Scott Peck who said there are two undeniable and inarguable truths. Number one is: The only way to stop is to stop. After all of the talk about our addictions, the things we do that we are sorry for, the only way to stop is in a decisive moment to stop doing that activity. There is a lot of discussion that goes on. A lot of the words are said trying to find some way we can get away with doing it while not changing anything. The only way to stop is to stop.

A Jewish man in Israel discovered that truth. Every day he would go to the Palestinian border with food. He would take it across to an elderly Palestinian couple and he would feed them. The soldiers at the gate would ask every day, "Why are you doing this?" What was even worse, they would discover in time that the couple he was feeding were persons who had lost their son. And even deeper, the Palestinian son whom they had lost in war was the same son who had killed his Israeli son. He knew enough to say, "The only way to stop is to stop." Somebody has to stop it. Reginald Denny and this Jewish man stopped.

The second undeniable truth that you cannot have a discussion about is:

II. Love makes the world go round.

Did Victor Hugo's *Les Miserables* really bring that to us? Jean Valjean comes to the Bishop's home and sees the silver there and takes it and is caught. And the Bishop saves him and gives him the worst burden of his life. He forgives him right on the spot. Valjean's entire life is haunted after that by seeking to find that appropriate place where he can give away that kind of love.

Most of the New Testament has been written by the apostle Paul. Have you ever stopped to think of what a gross character he was before his conversion? The one who gave us the most of what we call the "word of God" in the New Testament was killing and persecuting Christians. Later on he would give some terrible understatements about what happened to him, especially on the road to Damascus. He would in time say something so boring as "the love of Christ constrains us." Thank God we have some persons who can give a parallel to it, someone who came after that to say that the love of Christ "leaves us no choice." Jean Valjean knew that. In the mystery of being forgiven we have no choice but to find that incendiary moment in life that we might be called up to do the same even though in any given moment we don't feel like doing it.

Another one who has shown us the love of Christ was Terry Anderson. Everyone was excited about his release from his captors in Lebanon. They were shocked when he came to the news conference. The first question from the news people: "What would you like to have done to your captors?" It was the revenge question. His answer shocked and left them silent. "It isn't what I would like. I am a Catholic. I have been taught as a Christian that I must forgive." Silence. They didn't know how to ask more of him.

Frederick Buechner said:

> *When somebody you have wronged forgives you, you are spared the dull and self-diminishing throb of a guilty conscience. When you forgive someone who has wronged you, you are spared the dismal corrosion of bitterness and wounded pride for both parties. Forgiveness means the freedom again to be at peace inside your own skin and to be glad in each other's presence.*

It hurts and heals all in the same moment. We have known that, haven't we?

The word of God cuts and calms all at the same time. The word that helps hurts. It calms us and cuts us deeply.

There is the Jewish story about a man named Abraham who found a beggar and invited him into his home to feed him. The beggar just kept cursing him and being rude. Finally, Abraham kicked him out, saying, "I don't need this." And that night when Abraham went to speak to God in his prayers, he heard the voice of God saying, "This man you kicked out has cursed me for fifty years, and yet I have given him food to eat every day. Could you not put up with him for just a single meal on my behalf?"

There was a Zen school in Japan. They were training young boys in the discipline of meditation. The boys had been taken into seclusion. Among the boys there was one who kept stealing. So the boys finally put together a petition and came to the headmaster and stood there and said, "We are threatening right now to leave because we can't stand this kid any longer." The Zen master, who was so wise, approached them, looked at them, and said, "You are wise brothers. You are very wise. You are wise because you know the difference between right and wrong. You may go somewhere else to study if you wish, but this poor brother does not even know right from wrong. Who will teach him if I do not? I am going to keep him here even if all the rest of you leave." The story goes that a torrent of tears cleansed the face of that boy who had stolen, and the desire to steal was banished from him forever in that decisive moment.

I know a very sharp person in southern California who gave me a gift at Christmastime — a very interesting book. It is called *A Ranking of the 100 Most Influential People in History*. It is intriguing because of the criteria stated in it. The criteria, and you have to be careful, is that they must be persons who have influenced the **daily lives of people and also people in the world right now**. Jesus came in third. Some in the Christian community were upset. Jesus came in third and a rather distant third at that. Now remember the criteria: "who has influenced the most number of people even to this present day." Mohammed came in first, given the fact that that particular faith tradition would have more influence on the daily activities of its people. The second was Sir Isaac Newton. His influence would have to do with our worldview and how we see things differently in the world. But the third was Jesus, and we need to stay with this fact for just a moment. Right under the paragraph that talked about Jesus, it lifted up the text that is in front of us today: "Love your enemies"; "Turn the other cheek." And the people who put the book together said that anyplace you go in the Christian community throughout the world, you will find it self-evidently true that this is *not* a main belief that Christians live up to. They just don't do it, and we know that to be true. The writer said if they had found permeated in the Christian community that they were so familiar with these words and in support of each other carrying out those words on a daily basis and that the Christian people actually did this, without a shadow of a doubt Jesus would have been in first place. The thing that is to be our hallmark in the Church is our hobby, not a daily way of life.

III. When holding prisoners, make sure to prepare two cells.

If you are interested in holding prisoners in your life make sure to create two cells. Any clergy who would be honest with you will tell you that people often come to them. We clergy know the bottom line when they come into the office: "I just hate this. I just can't do it." A lot of sympathy needs to be given to them, both in primary and secondary emotions. I sat in a courtroom with parents whose daughter was accused of murder and found guilty. I have sat with the parents of children who were killed. There is intense pain in both places that is not easily healed. To talk about forgiveness casually goes right out the window when you are there.

Most often forgiveness cannot be given because we have not forgiven ourselves.

I told you about my friend Glen. As a child, there was a time when he and his father, a minister, had the privilege of going to the home of Corrie ten Boom. You remember her as that lady who, during the Second World War, helped hide Jewish people. Right there in her living room, as Glen was sitting there, she told the story of that time right after the Second World War when she was preaching that we needed to forgive all people, even those who were holding others in oppression. The only hope in the world was going to be in God's forgiveness as seen in Jesus Christ. A former Nazi sat in the front row while she said that. He stood up afterward, came to her, extended his hand, and said, "I was among the Nazis, and I need your forgiveness, and I want to thank you for your forgiveness this night." He held out his hand to her and she started to sweat and shake all over. She could not reach out her hand, and finally a prayer came to her that was really a gift to herself. She said, "God, give me your forgiveness," knowing that only in receiving that forgiveness can you give it away. In that prayer she was able to reach out her trembling hand and begin a very long path, a path that will last our entire lives: forgiving our enemies as we have been forgiven. We hold prisoners to the same degree we hold ourselves prisoners.

So why love our enemies? The person who was making a joke of it said, "Because it will drive them crazy." Why love our enemies? Because most often we isolate in them our weaknesses and seek to kill in them what we cannot control in ourselves. John Shea also warned that once you start to love your enemy you are going to lose something that has really been good for you in your life. He said, "The terrible effect of seeing God in all people is that our enemies are taken from us. Enemies supply energy. When we wake each morning in a mode of anger and attack, we know we are alive. We are ready to go. But when we see the others having the same crimes we do, something shifts. The edge is off. There is a problem. The enemy is us. We must love them in their crimes as we are loved in our crimes. This is not mental gymnastics. This is simply what the heart that loves God chooses to see."

Fred Craddock tells an imaginary story of Jesus after his death and resurrection. He has this window of opportunity to be with the persons who have loved him and also deserted him. There are times they are eating together. There are informal moments. There is no big plan for the future. There is simple sharing. Craddock has Jesus poking around the fire after breakfast one morning. One of the women who saw the cross and saw everything that happened there is agonizing over it. She says, "Jesus, they were so terrible to you. We were there. It was so awful. Jesus, you were a victim. I don't like the idea of you being a victim." Then she finally says, "They took your life." And Jesus, not even looking up, just poking in the fire, says with a victorious half smile, "They didn't take my life. I gave it."

Jesus said, "Love your enemies. Do good. Expecting nothing in return, your reward will be great, and you will be children of the most high."

I had a dream the other night. Actually it was more of a nightmare. I was preaching this sermon, using this text. Someone in the back row came up to the front and stood right next to the pulpit and wanted to interrogate me about this text. "Now tell me, Dick. Tell me about this text. Do you live this out any better than we do?" In the dream I remember, and this is reality, too, I said, "Of course not. Of course not. What do you think I am doing here? The only reason I am in this pulpit is because one time I read in the book of Hebrews that the one whom we call our priest is the same one who participates in the various sins we preach against. When I read that as a very young man, I said, 'For that reason alone I can enter ministry.' As for perfection, you can forget it. I am the same as you are, no better." "Then, Dick, I have one question to leave you with, 'Why do you preach this message?'" And in the dream I remember saying to him that I have discovered that if we keep looking at this text that makes us so uncomfortable, if we keep reading it and confess in the presence of God how much we fail it, then someday without even knowing it, we will find ourselves living this word rather than discussing it. The day that you live this word out when it is needed most in the life of another will be at a moment that you are not even conscious you have done it.

Meanwhile, we stand, arms linked together, as we affirm: **"Love your enemies." Confess how much we fail it, and listen to the voice of God that nudges us slowly toward the goal.**

May God help us to come here as often as we need to until that distant word is lived inside us without our even knowing it. For it is in that moment that the kingdom we have yearned for will come to us in a little sliver, and in that moment it will be enough for us to know love at the deepest level. May God grant us courage to come together until that happens to us. Amen.

Getting The Face We Deserve

The Transfiguration Of The Lord   Luke 9:28-36 (37-43, 51)
(Last Sunday After The Epiphany)

It has been advised that we always approach God quietly because God speaks in a whisper. While we are busy getting more of what we have enough of, while we are so noisy as a society, we don't hear the voice of God because we've been too loud. We must learn to receive God's whispering voice. The season of silence is the season of Lent which begins this week, but we're not into that season yet. We're in a season of bright light, the end of Epiphany.

In the Old Testament Moses goes up on the mountaintop, meets the face of God, and brightness shines on his face. He is a reflection of God's light. It's so bad that he has to wear something over his face because he blinds his friends. In the New Testament there is the story of Jesus, with Peter, James, and John on the mountaintop. Moses and Elijah appear; the lights come on. There's good news and there's bad news in the light of God shining on us. The good news is it gives us enough light for taking the next step in life. The bad news is that I am revealed for who I am when the light of God goes on, and there's no place for me to hide. And for me, sometimes, that's bad news. But Jesus, Peter, James, and John in the midst of the light begin to worship. They then do the Protestant thing and form a committee and immediately get into an argument about what they should do on the mountaintop. And then, the miracle comes. They hear the voice of God and they drop immediately into silence. That's the only time you can hear God because God speaks in a whisper, and we must be silent.

What we really learn out of this is that we can't *make* a religious experience. You know there's no phonier person in society, there's nothing more ridiculous in society, than anyone inside or outside the Church who tries to create a religious experience. Think of the most intimate moments in your life when you've felt closest to God. Just know that no one could have maneuvered that. No one could have created it. We can't create a religious experience. We can only come to God in silence. God does not know how to come to us except in that way.

Then the last verse. We jump a whole section. This is the axis mundi, i.e., the place around which everything revolves in the life of Jesus. It's the most important verse in the Gospel of Luke. "And Jesus sets his face toward Jerusalem." He made that decision that he would face opposition, hostility and finally death rather than head off to Egypt. That decision was to catapult him in a direction from which he could not run. Mystical experience is a gift in daily life that enables us to face whatever we need to face.

I'm going to look in two directions: the first, **that we face in,** to take a good look at ourselves. It's really time to do that, to face in, to really look at ourselves. It is a hard thing to do.

A mother in her mid-thirties died, leaving two little boys with their father. The funeral was over and they went home. It was bedtime. One of the little boys came tugging at his dad's blanket; he said he couldn't sleep.

"Can I come in here?"

"Yes, you can."

The lights are finally off. Then a voice comes from the dark. "Daddy, are you facing me? Are you facing toward me?"

"Yes, I am."

"I think then I can make it through the night."

In that abandoned child, his story is our story. The greatest hope we have is to keep looking to the face of the Holy One, who takes us away from nothing in life, but promises to go with us through all things. That source will be the final source that will get us through everything that we need to get through in this life. We learn that lesson late.

The Aborigines in Canada are in charge of being tour guides around the National Park. A lot of people visit there and many ask some curious questions about the Aborigines. One day a visitor asked, "What are we going to see once we get up on the mountaintop? I'm not sure if I want to go on this trip. What are we going to see?" And the guide rightly said, "It depends on what God will show you." It depends also on how much activity is going on inside you, how much sound is going on around you. It depends on what God will show you. He really is saying, "It depends on what you are willing to face." The blessing that finally comes to us in the Church is dependent on how much of ourselves we are willing to look at.

I like the story of Jesus being born, because it's one time you get a little bit of detail. Did you ever notice how the Bible is so bereft of any details? We all read it and say, "Gee, I need a few more details here. Why didn't somebody fill in the details?" We come here all the time and never get over that complaint. Once in a while, you get some data — some fish and loaves. They give a number. That's helpful. So here we finally get some details. At the time that Jesus came into the world, Caesar Augustus intended for all the world to be enrolled. That's a fancy way of saying that everybody had to go where they were born and sign up. Caesar was doing this new database. He was bringing all the names together. While the government was interested in data, and collecting it, God blessed the world with One who calls us to look inward. We're changed by One who couldn't care less about data, but who invites us to look low enough into a manger and find in that lowly solitude everything that we've been looking for in the wrong places.

I've read a lot about the superhighway of information. I keep asking, "How's this going to help me along the way?" I've come to the rapid conclusion that the superhighway of information will provide you with a lot of data, but it won't get you God. Sometimes we get fooled into thinking that by having the ability to hook up with other people, we're really discovering the fellowship of the church that can only be experienced face to face. God blesses not in data but in sacred story. "And Jesus set his face toward Jerusalem." And so we set our faces to look inward.

Abraham Lincoln was given the name of a man to serve on his cabinet. Lincoln immediately and abruptly said, "I don't want him." He was asked, "Why?" He said, "I don't like his face." Now if you really look at a picture of Lincoln, he didn't have a lot to talk about. As a matter of fact, one of the nasty things in one of his early campaigns was that people made fun of how ugly he was. He would confess, "I don't know why any woman would ever want me." And so he suffered with that. But he was looking in a different direction. His advisor came to him and rightly said, "President Lincoln, a human is not responsible for his face." Lincoln said, "Every person over forty is responsible for his face." It's up to us to find out what that might mean. To express the same thought someone said, "At fifty you get the face you deserve."

I met a photographer in San Francisco. He takes wonderful black and white pictures of famous people. They have that Ansel Adams look to them. I asked him about his work and he said the most interesting thing. He said, "I have discovered in my studio that after 25 years of age, attractiveness becomes increasingly a dimension of the personality rather than of the body."

"And Jesus set his face toward Jerusalem." He invites us to face inward and take a good look at ourselves. Besides facing in, **we need to face up.** We need to face up to how far we miss the kingdom even though we confess and say that we're aiming directly toward it. We need to face up to the fact that most often there's more harm done than good in the name of religion. Sometimes in moments when we get discouraged, we ask ourselves, "Well, where else can we go to serve God in a better way?"

Madeleine L'Engle was asked that question one time. She was working in a church in New York City as the artist and writer in residence. Someone came to her and said, "What do you think of the church?" She said, "Oh, the church! It's awful, but it's all we've got." Some days people will tell you, "If we could go any other place to serve God in a better dimension, we would." But we keep coming back to this place that can both hurt us and help us all on the same Sunday. We keep coming back to this place that is meant to be wrestled like the angel in the Old Testament until we pin it down to do more good than harm. You see, Jesus came not to demand faith nor to create a religion; but to let us know, in the name of God, how much faith God has in us. That was his message. And yet why is it that that message so often comes out as judgment and not as One who tenaciously seeks us, not with judgment, but with love?

We come from a long tradition of bright lights. We see it in the Old Testament. It's the bright face of Moses. Today we have Jesus in the New Testament. And Jesus does say in the Gospel of John, "I am the light of the world." Then he says he is going to be leaving. Then he says, "You're the light of the world." He entrusts to us this light and asks us to take it forward. Instead, the opposite often happens.

There's a man who came to visit here six months ago who didn't choose to join the church because he didn't think he belonged here. His wife still comes, but he didn't want to because he knew that he was an agnostic. Yet he came back and I was able to communicate to him that he belonged here because there are many people sitting here that are Christian indeed, and agnostic a little. He came here and recognized that this was the place to bring whatever faith he had or didn't have. He said to me that he believes in that God revealed by Jesus. He said he's horrified at much Biblical literature and mystified by most of it. I again told him, "You're in good company." And when I saw his face, I remembered this: "There is more faith in honest doubt than in all of the creeds of the Church." That would seem to be what we in this congregation believe. That's one thing he wanted to tell me. The next thing he wanted to tell me is that his cancer had flared up again.

A year ago my dad died. During the last stage of his illness, we gave him as much medication as possible to keep him away from the pain. So it is with this man. They're trying to keep the pain away from him. Last week, there was a neighbor who went to call on him. He said that he is a Christian and that he is religious. Then the neighbor brought out a tape recorder and played tapes for this dazed man who belongs to us. He was told that unless he set a certain formula about believing in Jesus, he was doomed beyond this world. At this, my friend simply looked up with dazed and glazed eyes and saw only his friend, and didn't even hear the words. Thank God! He looked at his friend, who came to save him by putting him through a useless formula, and he motioned toward his new golf club and said, "Take this, my friend, because I won't be able to use it any longer."

I would ask you a simple question: where do you see the Christian faith in that encounter, in the one who comes to pronounce judgment or the one who in honest doubt loves even in the shadow of his own death? I imagine that there have been times you've wondered why the Church doesn't get the attention in this culture that you believe it ought to have. There will be a reformation when instead of giving judgment we give the good news that God handed off to us in Jesus Christ. And it is at that moment that we need to see the light that was shining on the face of Jesus Christ who called us to love.

When you come into my office, there is a story of the prodigal son in a picture hanging on the wall. The reason that it is there, and I think it ought to be in every counselor's office, is because it is everybody's story. Was there not some moment in your life when you were arrogant? I can't speak for you, so I'll just speak for me. I remember a time in my life when I was arrogant. I came to those in charge and said, "Give me what belongs to me," even though I didn't deserve it. I can remember a time when I squandered my life and my means and I just wasn't paying attention to the gifts that God had set before me. I can remember being very regretful of things I'd said and done, just like the prodigal child. All of us have to come to that place in ourselves where we are forced to face ourselves. And from it we get the true picture of God who spots the child in the distance and runs to him. His shoes are off now. He's running to embrace the child. "This is my son who was lost. Now he is found." What's the business of God? He's in the lost business. God seeks the lost, not with reprimand, but with love. When the church lives like that, I'm telling you, the human family has discovered fire a second time. Jesus sets his face toward

Jerusalem, and it is time for us to **face in** and to **face up** until we are changed by the light that was shining on the face of Jesus Christ.

People come to me and ask the questions, "How can I be changed? How do you get changed? What changes you in life, Dick? How do we change in the human family?" It reminds me of the Jewish story of a man who was lost in the forest. Suddenly there was lightning, and the Hasidim would say, "When that lightning comes, the fool is the one who looks to the sky and the lightning. The wise person is the one who looks at the path that is illuminated in the little flashes that are symbolic of the presence of God." He comes in little flashing moments. Those little moments don't stay around a long time but they're enough to keep us going. We are changed by flashes of light, I think, as we see the light shining on the face of Jesus Christ.

So, what changes us? A guru in India, a holy man, is sitting by the water. He sees a scorpion caught in a thicket. He puts his hand down in the thicket. He gets stung. He does it twice, three, four times more. He's stung four times. There's a student standing over to the side who comes running and says, "You fool! Why are you doing that? Every time you put your hand down there, you're going to get stung. You need to stop doing that." And the guru says to the student, "Because it is the nature of the scorpion to sting, should I change my nature which is to save?"

God reaches out. Most of the time we're too noisy or too busy getting more of what we have enough of, or we're looking for God in all the wrong places. God continues to reach out. Every once in a while, when we dare to be silent, the hand of God touches us in a mysterious way. The next time that happens to you, will you notice that hand and how it has been stung? Notice the marks. God still reaches out to us. He knows no other way than to keep coming to us in love rather than judgment. It is that scratched, stung, and still loving hand that changes us.

May God bless us in the church and in our lives with each other as we share that love and are found by the mystery of the light that was shining on the face of Jesus Christ. Amen.

Books In This Cycle C Series

Gospel Set

Sermons For Advent/Christmas/Epiphany
Deep Joy For A Shallow World
Richard A. Wing

Sermons For Lent/Easter
Taking The Risk Out Of Dying
Lee Griess

Sermons For Pentecost I
The Chain Of Command
Alexander H. Wales

Sermons For Pentecost II
All Stirred Up
Richard W. Patt

Sermons For Pentecost III
Good News Among The Rubble
J. Will Ormond

First Lesson Set

Sermons For Advent/Christmas/Epiphany
Where Is God In All This?
Tony Everett

Sermons For Lent/Easter
Returning To God
Douglas J. Deuel

Sermons For Pentecost I
How Long Will You Limp?
Carlyle Fielding Stewart, III

Sermons For Pentecost II
Lord, Send The Wind
James McLemore

Sermons For Pentecost III
Buying Swamp Land For God
Robert P. Hines, Jr.